THANK GOD I GOT POLIO

THANK GOD I GOT POLIO

A LIFE OF ADVENTURE AND THE ADVENTURE OF LIFE

Wayne Raffesberger

Waterside Productions

Printed in the United States of America

Cover design by Ken Fraser, Impact Book Designs

Photo credits— Front cover: the author on top of the Matterhorn. Back cover: top of page, the author on top of Mt. Kilimanjaro; bottom of page, the author at the base of Kilimanjaro after completion of the climb. All photos by the author.

First Printing, 2021

ISBN-13: 978-1-956503-14-2 print edition
ISBN-13: 978-1-956503-15-9 ebook edition

Waterside Productions
2055 Oxford Ave
Cardiff, CA 92007
www.waterside.com

"I dream of journeys repeatedly ..."

—Theodore Roethke, *The Far Field*

DEDICATION

It's been the journey of a lifetime. This book is dedicated to all those who helped me along that journey: my friends and family, the doctors and nurses who cared for me, my wife, Kaye, for her understanding and support during the long writing process, and to my big brother, Glenn, for the best horsey ride ever. Finally, to anyone struggling with life's challenges. If I have encouraged or inspired you in any way, it's all been worth it.

TABLE OF CONTENTS

INTRODUCTION

I sat alone in the small campus library, occasionally glancing outside at the snowy ground and the dark German forest beyond. I tried to read background for my class in the philosophy of Friedrich Nietzsche, but the difficulty of the material left me distracted. I had an uneasy feeling, too, as if someone, or something, was watching me.

Randomly flipping through other books, a line of poetry jumped out. "The wolf trots to and fro, the world lies deep in snow." I didn't note the author, and wondered why the line grabbed me. I sat back down, still pondering the meaning of the words.

When I looked through the window again, there he was. Moving back and forth at the edge of the woods and staring at me with a wicked grin—a wolf. Was it the same wolf who attacked me years before, devouring half of my leg? Was he back for more?

Would someone be there to save me this time?

CHAPTER 1

THE ADVENTURE BEGINS

One morning long ago, I woke up and fell out of bed.

It was October 1955. I was four years old, so it wasn't unusual for me to fall on the floor. Except this time, I couldn't get up. I tried to use my legs, but nothing happened.

My brother Glenn and I shared a room, and he heard me struggling. He rushed to my side, and though he was older, he wasn't strong enough to help me to my feet. I stayed on the cold, wooden floor wondering what was wrong while he went to wake our parents.

Dad came and lifted me back onto the bed. He looked at me and said something like, "Don't worry, you'll be fine." Then he disappeared. Glenn followed him, and I was left alone.

I sat on the bed, still wondering. I wasn't frightened or in pain, just bewildered. After a while, Glenn returned to tell me the amazing news that our parents were in our little kitchen, *crying*. That was incredible to us; we had never seen them cry before.

The mysterious sight had to be seen. Glenn said he could help. He sidled up to the bed, horsey style, and I crawled onto his back. Like the famous line from the movie *Boys Town*, "He ain't heavy ... he's my brother," he would get me there somehow.

I clung to his back as we moved through the small living room to the kitchen. We stayed in the doorway, staring at Mom and Dad. They were still crying, holding hands at the kitchen table and choking out words to each other. I couldn't understand why they were so distraught, or much of what they were saying, but they kept repeating a word I had never heard—*polio*.

Polio. From that moment forward, and for the rest of my life, that one word would dominate everything. How the world looked at me, how I looked at myself, and how, ultimately, it would motivate me to embrace it. To accept the very word that for most of my life was heartbreaking anathema.

For whatever reason, known only to God, polio ravaged my hometown of San Diego in the early 1950s. The city was not alone, of course, as thousands across the country fell to the dreaded disease. Scientists desperately raced to perfect vaccines and began to halt the spread of the scourge. Despite their efforts, though, many of us in San Diego contracted it in 1955.

Parents in America lived with a gnawing fear, as polio was more likely to attack children. An insidious disease—no one knew when, or where, or whom it would strike next. But everyone knew about it, and everyone was scared.

Mom and Dad knew that morning, too. They bundled up my two brothers and me and drove to the new Children's Hospital in town. That it even existed was the first miracle of my life. Children's had only opened a few months before, as a special polio ward for young victims. Without Children's, I probably would have been sent to a hospital in Los Angeles, a catastrophic outcome.

They placed me in a large room with several other boys. Doctors and nurses hovered about all day long, muttering in low voices to Mom and Dad. As darkness came on, the folks kissed me goodbye and promised to return the next day. Later, a nurse came by and pulled curtains around my bed. In the darkened room, a boy was crying. I don't remember if I cried, too.

CHAPTER 2

THE WOLF OF POLIO

The terrifying word polio is derived from *poliomyelitis*, a disease from the invasive poliovirus. When I was diagnosed, there were three types of the virus, all of which began in the gastrointestinal tract, and generally spread through fecal matter. Depending on the type of infection and the severity, some of the infected only experienced fever, headaches, temporary muscle weakness, and pain. Many suffered a far worse outcome—permanent destruction of nerve cells, leading ultimately to muscle atrophy and paralysis. And many, numbering in the thousands, succumbed to the paralysis.

America in the early 1950s struggled desperately to conquer polio. 1952 saw nearly 58,000 cases, the worst outbreak in the country's history. Twenty-one thousand of those cases resulted in some form of paralysis. Millions of families lived in fear that they—more specifically their children—might be next.

After years of research and testing, three different vaccine methodologies emerged. A disease that had frightened civilization since ancient times neared a cure. Dr. Jonas Salk developed the most prominent of the three. Announced to the world on April 12, 1955, the Salk vaccine consisted of a series of shots of an inactivated, or killed, poliovirus. The wolf of polio had stalked the nation for years, so the announcement caused a national sensation. Grown men wept with joy, politicians at the highest level shouted hosannas of praise, and ordinary parents everywhere prayed with gratitude that their children would now be safe.

A few years later, Albert Sabin produced a live virus vaccine, this one oral. It required only one dose for initial effectiveness against all three polio viruses, but needed three doses for maximum effect. The Sabin vaccine was inexpensive and relatively easy to administer. Ultimately, it became the standard polio vaccine utilized worldwide.

Controversy around these two primary types of vaccines had raged for years. Supporters of each methodology pointed out that it was possible to actually contract polio from the rival vaccine itself. Despite the national euphoria, a measure of doubt still lingered.

In 1955, though, the country had the Salk vaccine and finally, hope. San Diego in particular needed that hope, as hundreds of people in the city had contracted polio in just the previous two years.

Community leaders quickly organized a mass inoculation event. On April 16th, a coordinated team of 175 physicians, together with nurses and volunteers, administered the vaccine to 28,000 of the city's children, all on the same day. San Diego wasn't a very big city in those days, and that number in one day made national news.

Banner headlines in the local paper, *The San Diego Union*, trumpeted the accomplishment. At the time it was, "The world's first countywide inoculation against polio." One of the lead organizers of the effort was Dr. James MacLaggan, a member of the County Medical Society's polio advisory committee. Ironically, Dr. MacLaggan's son, Peter, and I became good friends many years later without me ever knowing about his father's work.

The Union extolled the herculean inoculation effort. "From the standpoint of the children," the paper declared, "it was a victory ... a great relief." That relief soon turned to grief when several inoculated children contracted polio. Just 11 days later, *The Union* headline read, "No reason for alarm, doctors stress; serum withdrawn after children contract disease."

Doubt spread about the Salk vaccine, despite the killed virus it contained. Many parents worried that their children would actually receive the poliovirus from the vaccine. In fact, several children who had been vaccinated on the 16th did contract polio, leading to a very real local "polio scare." Nationally, dozens of children who were similarly vaccinated contracted the disease, and a number of them died.

Federal health authorities temporarily withdrew the vaccine for new tests. Rumor and fear spread through the country. One prominent national media personality even labeled the vaccine a "killer." Officials desperately scrambled for answers while deciding what to do next.

The massive new testing ordered by the government revealed that all of the victims were children inoculated with vaccine from just one of the six labs nationally authorized to make it. The government halted production from that lab, and then lifted the total ban in early May. Inoculations resumed, but at a slower pace, as many parents were now deeply skeptical.

There were 29,000 cases of polio nationally in 1955. Doctors and health professionals agonized over how many of those cases could have been avoided if the vaccine had been more widely administered, or if more parents had not avoided the vaccine for fear of its possible consequences.

Still, just the existence of the vaccine that spring gave hope to millions of families where none existed before. *The Union* trumpeted that hope in a headline: "City mothers lose dread of summer," quoting one local leader of the March of Dimes. "Isn't this wonderful? There won't be any more dread of polio in summer from now on."

Summer had been associated with the polio virus seemingly forever, to the point that many called it polio season. Researchers struggled to learn exactly how the virus was transmitted, but generally believed it had something to do with cleanliness. Speculation centered on the heat of summer exacerbating dirty conditions, leading to a more virulent virus. Warm summer weather certainly meant more human interaction, particularly among children. The disease definitely affected children more than adults, and boys more than girls. Some experts considered polio contagious even through just human contact or sneezing.

It was contagious, of course, but not through mere touching or sneezing. The contagion came from infected fecal matter, which explained why the disease predominantly affected children. Children, being children, never had the same sanitary habits as adults. It also explained why swimming pools became off limits in cities across the country. Health officials everywhere, struggling to understand exactly how it spread, repeated the mantra of "Avoid public swimming pools."

Our tiny rented house sat in a lower-income neighborhood in east San Diego. There were no public swimming pools nearby, and few anywhere in what was then not a wealthy city. As a four-year old, I didn't even know how to swim, and had never been in a swimming pool.

The older boy several doors away, though, had something special in his front yard—a large surplus military life raft, filled with water from a garden

5

hose. To all of us neighborhood kids, it seemed enormous, and like a swimming pool. We splashed around with each other all that hot summer, and no one ever thought about anything but fun. A few months later, I contracted polio.

Federal public health officials announced plans to inoculate 57 million children. There is no way to know how many children were saved through the massive inoculation efforts against the scourge of what one expert called, "the most feared disease of the twentieth century." What I do know is that I wasn't one of them.

I could never state with any certainty that I came down with the infection from that raft. Reflecting back on that distant time, though, it's all that makes sense. Before my parents passed away, I discussed my theory with Mom. She couldn't remember the raft. I also asked her for the first and only time in my life, "Was I ever vaccinated?" "No," she said, "we were afraid of the vaccine." I left it at that and never mentioned the subject again. I could only imagine the anguish they must have felt, crying at the kitchen table that fateful morning, realizing the consequences of their decision.

CHAPTER 3

THE FIRST DAY OF THE REST OF MY LIFE

Waking up the first morning at Children's Hospital began my lifelong odyssey. To say that it was "the first day of the rest of my life," as the old cliché goes, would be quite the understatement. I would never again be able to run without great difficulty, or even take a single step without first consciously remembering how to walk. In fact, as the doctors later told my parents, there was no certainty I would ever walk again.

Children's had only opened a few months before I arrived. Now a world-class pediatric hospital and known as Rady Children's Hospital, it was first created as just a polio ward for afflicted children. The uncertainty of the polio contagion led officials to quarantine us in a ward, isolated from all others.

Sunlight streamed through the windows that early October morning when the nurses scurried about, pulling back curtains and the drapes around each bed. Some of the children began to cry out for their parents. Nurses comforted the kids, and later wheeled in breakfast. Doctors and hospital staff came and went, administering antibiotic shots in the vague hope that those would somehow help, taking temperatures, and offering assurances to the shell-shocked parents who began to fill the room. Many of those parents cried along with their children.

All day I waited, alone, for Mom and Dad. Our family didn't have a lot of money and could only afford one used old car, so a visit had to wait until Dad came home from work and picked up Mom. His career as an engineer was just getting started, and Mom worked as a homemaker, taking care of my brothers and me. When evening came and they arrived, they were upbeat, unlike most of the other parents. They said things like "you'll be well, soon, Wayne," and "you're going to be home soon, too."

I stayed there in the hospital bed day after day, unable to walk, waiting for them to come for their daily visit. The days turned into weeks, and the weeks into months, and I wasn't getting any better. There is still no cure for the disease, only inoculation.

There was comfort for those affected, though, and Children's provided that in an enormous way. I remember the love and kindness showered on me by the doctors and nurses to this day. How different my life would have turned out had Children's not existed. The nearest other pediatric hospital was in Los Angeles, hours away by car. My life and my parents' lives would have been completely disrupted, much more so than they already were by my contracting the disease.

Whether it was the hospital care, the drugs they gave me, the rest, or divine intervention, the virus eventually stopped ravaging my body. The wolf had finished eating. But not before permanent damage was done. There are three types of paralytic polio, and I clearly had one of them—spinal, a viral invasion of the motor neurons in the spinal column. When the virus destroyed the nerve cells, muscles no longer received signals from the brain or the spinal column. Without that stimulation, the muscles weakened, atrophied, and ultimately become completely paralyzed and dead.

After a few weeks, the doctors considered it safe for me to be out of bed. Nurses rolled me in a wheelchair daily to an exercise room. There, they helped me to my feet between two parallel bars, where I tried endlessly, and unsuccessfully, to walk. I never quit trying, though. I knew that somehow, someway, I would walk again.

Mom and Dad refused to believe that the muscles wouldn't come back. They thought that once I was home and back exercising again, the muscles would return. To encourage me that better days were ahead, they brought me a silver dollar on every visit. When the silver dollars became an enormous pile beside my hospital bed, they asked me what I wanted to do with my little treasure. I told them that all I wanted was to be like the other kids—to be able to play outside again. To be normal. I said I wanted a swing set for the backyard. "Would the money be enough?" I asked. Of course it would, they assured me. For years, that swing set was my most prized possession.

CHAPTER 4

HOME FOR THE HOLIDAYS

Despite the doctors' reluctance, Mom and Dad insisted on bringing me home for Christmas. Excitement overwhelmed me as they rolled my wheelchair out of the hospital, heading home after nearly three months alone in the ward. My grandmother even rode the Greyhound bus all the way from Wisconsin to help out with the burden that I would be at home. I remember well the indescribable bliss of simply being home, back again playing with my brothers. Hearing their laughter, enjoying meals with the family, and sleeping in my own bed. Despite everything, it was probably the best Christmas of my life.

Spinal polio tended to afflict children with paralysis in one lower limb, and I was no different. It attacked only my left leg, from the hip and buttock all the way to the foot. They fitted me with a steel brace that covered the entire leg, but it wasn't very effective. Too weak to walk, I mostly moved around in the wheelchair. To walk, the brace had to be locked in a straight position. It really wasn't walking at all—I dragged the one immobilized leg behind me. When I got tired and sat down, the leg would extend straight out until an adult came along strong enough to release the lock and let the knee bend. If I wanted to move, I had to wait for someone else to lock it in position again. Without that, I would stand up and immediately fall over.

My life started over. From that time forward, everything would be about trying to overcome somehow the damage the wolf of polio had done to my body. A van from Children's showed up at our house several times a week to transport me back to the hospital for physical therapy. While there, I performed endless repetitions of trying to walk between the parallel bars without a brace, along with various other exercises. Although walking with the brace was awkward and difficult, I dutifully tried to march everywhere.

Children's introduced me to the man who would one day help me walk without braces, Dr. Walter Carpenter. Dr. Carpenter was an early member of the Foundation for Infantile Paralysis, the organization that started the March of Dimes, and a local leader in the fight against polio. For nearly 10 years he treated me, performing multiple operations on my leg, monitoring my progress at regular visits, and offering warmth and encouragement. I can still see his bald head, glasses, and avuncular face to this day, smiling at me as I staggered toward him in his office while he watched my attempts at walking for signs of progress or deterioration.

He was an enormous part of why I can walk today. It didn't occur to me as young, full-of-myself boy and young man to go back and thank him and Children's for what they did for me. That thought came to me many years later. When it did, it consumed me. But sadly, too late to tell him in person.

CHAPTER 5

THE COMEBACK KID

By 1956, I was five years old. We lived in a new tract house in the suburbs, with my new swing set proudly erected in the backyard, shared with neighborhood kids. On it, I could climb and play just like a "normal" child.

I endured the first of my surgeries during that time. Chunks of bone were cut out of one part of the withered leg and inserted in other parts in order to arrest warped growth. After healing from the procedure, my fondest wish came true. The doctors allowed me to transition from a hip brace to one that only extended from my foot to just below my knee. What a great moment, without so much extra weight to drag around.

The brace appeared obvious to anyone looking at me, though, regardless of its size. One night, Mom, my brothers, and I were down at San Diego's then little airport terminal, waiting for Dad to arrive from a business flight. Two strange men who had arrived on an earlier flight walked past us with their baggage—golf clubs. Noticing my leg and brace sticking out, they came over to say hi. Mom instantly knew their tanned, handsome faces and was thrilled. I screamed out, crying in fear of the strangers, despite their smiling attempts to cheer me up. The two men were Bob Hope and Bing Crosby, in town to play a little golf.

Mom and Dad were still convinced that with enough exercise, the atrophied, dead muscles would somehow revive. They bought little weights that attached to my shoe and had me perform endless leg lifts. I eagerly did the exercise, also believing that it would work. They tried everything, even taking me for massages from an older German immigrant couple, whose old-world technique consisted of vigorous massage and puddles of rubbing alcohol. I can smell that rubbing alcohol to this day. None of it worked. Once the muscles are dead, they're dead forever. The only hope was more surgery and building up what muscles survived.

Our family went to church every Sunday, at St. Luke's Lutheran Church in La Mesa, a San Diego suburb. When I first contracted the disease, the church bulletin asked the entire congregation to pray for me. At my young age, I knew what prayer was, even if I was too young to understand the bigger concept of religion. Mom taught me a special prayer and urged me to repeat it regularly. So, every night, and for years to come, the last thing I would do before falling asleep was to pray to God that he would make my leg just like the other one. And, every morning, I woke up and pulled the covers back, only to discover that the prayer had not been answered. Regardless of my disappointment, I knew I was on the way back, getting stronger every day.

CHAPTER 6

TRYING TO BE NORMAL

As I grew a little older, my main focus became playing and exercising, doing anything to build up my body. All I wanted was to be like the other kids. That would never really be possible as long as a steel brace was attached to my left leg, dragging along behind me.

Reminders of the brace were everywhere. At my kindergarten school, the teacher had a practice of asking each student who came to class with new shoes to stand up and walk in front of the room to see if the new shoes squeaked. One day she noticed that I had new shoes, and asked me to do the walk. I went up to her and whispered that my brace always squeaked, so this maybe didn't make sense. She loudly announced to the class that I had a brace that squeaked, and had me walk anyway. I stumbled around in front of them, wondering why.

The older girl next door gave me a genuine sense of freedom when she taught me to ride a bike. It was bliss to travel around our neighborhood with mobility, and without the stares and whispers that followed me everywhere when I walked. I have ridden a bike almost constantly from that day until now.

Swimming provided another outlet that allowed me to feel normal. Mom began taking me to lessons at a local indoor YMCA pool. I wasn't good at first, but the instructor persisted, encouraging me with her warmth and smile. Every time I finished splashing around, there she was pool-side saying, "You're doing great, Wayne."

I loved being in the water where I had no brace and no limp, and in later years, swam well enough to be on my high school swim team. I didn't know it at the time, but the instructor was the mother of Dennis Hopper, the actor, and ultimately, a fellow alumnus of the same high school, Helix, in La Mesa.

The constant play and exercise helped, but only to a point. What muscles were left improved a bit, but not much was left. My left buttock was half of normal size, the back of my thigh and the calf were gone, and my misshapen foot barely worked. At the end of my growing cycle, the leg ended up three inches shorter than the other one. I didn't like to look at it myself, and couldn't bear to have others staring at it.

I developed an almost silly routine to measure my physical progress. Every morning, I stood up to put on my pants, first standing on my good leg. Then, I would try to stand on the weak leg to handle the other pant leg, and fall over onto the floor. I kept up the routine every morning, year after year. And for many years, I just continued falling over, too weak to stand on that leg, but determined to keep trying.

I was, of course, too young to understand that those were my own Sisyphean moments. Sisyphus endlessly pushing his rock up the hill, only to ultimately fail near the top, the rock rolling back to the bottom. Sisyphus following, then beginning the endless struggle all over again, and again.

CHAPTER 7
CHILDREN CAN BE CRUEL

Children can indeed be cruel. Most of the time, that cruelty is inadvertent, born of naivete. Simply too young to understand the ramifications of what they say or do. Sometimes, though, other children can be deliberately vicious and cruel. For inexplicable reasons, they turn meanness into a sport. As I progressed through elementary school, I experienced both varieties.

We moved in 1958 to a new neighborhood in La Mesa, one that had lots of other kids. I was seven years old. The neighbors were friendly, and my brothers and I played together with their kids year-round. Hikes in the local hills, pick-up sports games at the local junior high school, hide-and-seek between houses, and a pool in our backyard. A *Mayberry, R.F.D.* kind of life.

The trouble began when I left the neighborhood. And often, at my own elementary school. I could roll my bike down the hill to school, but after that, on foot and exposed. Because I was new to that school in the second grade, some of the students that didn't know me from before were the worst.

Two of them in particular cackled like the popular cartoon characters Heckel and Jeckel, nasty little crows. "False foot," they yelled on the playground at recess. Followed me around shouting words like "gimpy." Why, I never knew. I had never done or said anything to them in the short time I had been enrolled at the school. Decades later, authorities arrested one of the two boys for making the poison ricin, and threatening to send it out to kill people. He is still in federal prison to this day, and honestly, when I heard of his arrest, all I could think of was, *yes, he was always evil.*

There were many other things said back then, but to me they were completely overshadowed by the singular day of my life to that point. The doctors decided that after three long years, I no longer needed to wear the brace. Ecstasy. I was free to walk alone; not well, and with a pronounced limp, but I could walk by myself. No more waking up and strapping on the cold steel of the brace. No more of the worn leather straps rubbing my skin raw. Pure bliss.

Those were years when two of the most popular TV shows in America were *The Real McCoys* and *Gunsmoke.* I watched those shows with my family like much of the country, but two characters in particular stood out to me. Dennis Weaver's character, Chester, in *Gunsmoke* and Walter Brennen's character of Grandpa McCoy in *The Real McCoys.* In both roles, the script called for the character to have a severe limp. God, how I hated those characters.

Inevitably, the morning after the shows aired, I would be at school or some other place and someone would call me Chester, or the Real McCoy, or just start imitating the characters' exaggerated limps. I remember one day when my brothers and I were walking along the sidewalk of a busy commercial street in town. An older boy, whom I recognized, was walking toward us. As soon as he saw me, he assumed the gait of Chester, marching past us with a pronounced limp and a dirty smirk.

More imaginative taunts were "hop-a-long," and "step-and-a-half." Heard them all. Sometimes the taunters were complete strangers, and many times they knew me. In retrospect, I think that at least some of them simply thought in their naivete that they were being funny, not mean, and that I would think so, too. I never did. It always hurt, wounding me deeply.

Two words also wounded me. The word polio made me literally cringe. I could not bear to hear it or think about it, repressing it to a dark corner of my mind. And the word cripple, my own personal "C-word," pained me like nothing else. I was called a cripple to my face so many times I couldn't possibly remember them all. I hate that word to this day.

As always, boys would gather together at recess or after school for pick-up games of any sport. We were no different, circling around to chose sides, with those designated as captains alternating their picks. Almost without exception, they picked me last. I understood why, but quietly never accepted it.

One incident in sixth grade remains seared into my mind. Another boy and I had an argument, which escalated into name calling, and a general agreement that we hated each other. A day or two later, we were in class and I noticed a piece of paper being passed around. When it came to me, I stared in stunned disbelief. The other boy was an excellent artist, and had drawn a picture of me supine. He depicted my left leg as that of a skeleton, encased in an open coffin.

CHAPTER 8

LITTLE LEAGUE

Baseball enthralled me, the only sport I was good at, besides swimming, of course. You get good at swimming when you have a backyard pool. I played ball constantly, with neighborhood kids, with my brothers, throwing against a wall alone, and in Little League. Despite my inability to run well, I could still play ball. I played the positions where I didn't have to run: pitcher and first base.

I loved Little League. My brothers and all of my friends played. Dad coached, and Mom cheered in the stands. With endless practice, I became a pretty good pitcher. I wanted the ball, wanted to lead my team. Frankly, I liked being the center of attention. On the mound, my leg didn't matter as much, my arm did. I competed as hard as I could, never asked for special consideration, and none was given.

We hung an old blanket on a big wooden fence in the backyard, and I would come home from school and throw by myself. Day after day, until I could place the ball wherever I wanted it. When Dad came home from his engineering job, I begged him to come outside and toss the ball with me across the street. Frequently, he loosened his tie, rolled up the sleeves on his white shirt, and indulged me. The movie *Field of Dreams* has a similar scene where the character played by Kevin Costner asks his Dad to play a little catch. When my wife, Kaye, and I went to see the movie, she couldn't understand why I was quietly choking up in the darkened theater as that scene evolved.

Little League only lasts until the end of elementary school, or 12 years old. After that, it's Pony League, played on a much bigger field and with players wearing steel cleats. When spring approached, I fully expected to go down to the field and sign up to play.

That anticipation crashed when my parents called me into the living room and said that we needed to talk. I could tell by their tone that nothing good was coming. They told me how happy they were that I had made so much physical progress over the years. Then they added that we couldn't risk my leg getting injured, maybe spiked by those steel cleats and permanently ruined. The leg that had been surgically rebuilt and nurtured back into some semblance of normal. They wouldn't permit me to play baseball again. I didn't agree with them, but had no choice other than to move on from one of the saddest days of my young life.

Over the next two years, I frequently rode my bike down the hill from home to the Pony League field to watch my buddies play. The field sat adjacent to the same Little League field where I learned the game I loved. I was always happy to see my friends play, but forlorn to think of how much I wanted to be on the field with them.

CHAPTER 9

SCHOOL DAYS

Junior high school offered a true adventure. Meeting new students, the different classes and teachers, having a locker, school dances; all of it so exotic compared to elementary school. During my two years, I excelled in classes, played saxophone in the concert band, got elected to the student council, served as one of the student newspaper editors, made many new friends, and generally enjoyed a good time. A good time, except when it came to gym class.

Gym class in seventh grade, wearing shorts, was the first time I ever had to display my leg to strangers. Staring, pointing, whispers, and laughs behind my back occurred constantly, leaving me in silent agony. Every change into my gym clothes filled me with shame and embarassment. I avoided that trauma whenever I swam in a pool other than ours, or went to the beach. I always carried my towel draped strategically in front of the leg, only dropping it at the water's edge.

They placed me in a special gym class called Adaptive P.E. There were disabled students in the class, and we were all called "adaptos" by other students. The pejorative term served as the butt of many school jokes. I couldn't understand why I was in the class instead of outside doing the regular gym-class things with my friends. I never thought of myself as disabled, ever.

I worked on my assigned exercises for the class one morning when an older boy walked in with a friend of his. The boy was angry about being in the class for his weight issues. He pointed at me, laughed at my leg, and said, "Can you believe they put me in here with him?"

I convinced the coaches the next year just to enroll me in regular gym class. It was a struggle to keep up, especially when they had us run laps around the dirt ballfields. I always finished last, far behind the others, but determined to finish.

One day, another boy whom I didn't know dropped back and ran alongside me. He insisted on telling me how lucky I was that I could even run at all, and how others had it much worse. I muttered some acknowledgment and he ran on. I never saw the boy again after that, and never knew him. I admitted to myself that he was right, but didn't need him to tell me. Was he a messenger sent from beyond to remind me to keep everything in perspective?

Because I was popular and outgoing, the kind of direct insults I experienced when younger were rare. But indirect ones continued, whether staring, the inadvertent remark, or the constant question, "What did you do to your leg?"

I remember a class when a teacher asked for an example of dark humor. An especially bright boy raised his hand to answer with an example. "It's like the joke about the boy who has a deformed hand, and he prays to God to make it like the other one. He wakes up, and both hands are deformed," he said. The class all laughed, even the teacher. I could only look out the window, alone with my thoughts, remembering my own prayer from earlier years, which obviously hadn't been answered.

About that time, I first heard a joke that I would hear constantly, and for many years to come. "That's about as funny as a rubber crutch in a polio ward," went the line. I'm sure that the young students and even adults who repeated it in my presence never thought about my experience, or in most cases, even knew. I never responded to hearing it, despite wanting to ask, "What would you know about a polio ward?" None of them ever knew what pain envisioning such a cruel scene caused me.

Near the end of seventh grade, school officials took me aside and suggested that I consider skipping eighth grade and proceed straight to high school. They either thought I really had nothing left to learn there, or they wanted to get rid of a precocious and sometimes annoying little bugger, or both. The idea intrigued me, so we began the process. I received the course book for the mandatory class in government, which I read at home and tested out of easily. Then they gave me a standard I.Q. test, and back came genius-level results. We agreed that I was ready, so they enrolled me in two summer-school classes at the local high school.

I did well in both classes until the doctors decided that I needed surgery one more time. Facing surgery again hurt, but so did having to drop those classes that I really enjoyed. I also regretted giving up the idea of skipping a grade, but rehabilitation of my leg that summer was far more important.

The multiple procedures Dr. Carpenter and the team at Children's Hospital performed included removing another chunk of bone from my shin and implanting it into my ankle joint, transplanting muscle from the underside of my foot onto the top of the big toe, and inserting a stabilizing rod into the big toe. They designed the procedures to keep my already deformed foot from deteriorating further and to give me at least some control of the ankle and big toe.

After many weeks in a walking cast, the moment came to remove it and test the rebuilt foot. I wondered during those weeks why the cast had a funny-looking extension beyond my big toe, which caused excruciating pain whenever I bumped it on anything. When the nurse finished cutting away everything, a cork protruded from the toe. She pulled it off to reveal the last 1/2 inch of a 2 and 1/2 inch nail, inserted straight into the toe. Without anything to numb the pain, she simply grabbed a pair of pliers and yanked the nail out. Mom heard my screams in the waiting room. I remember that pain today.

The miracle workers at Children's succeeded again. I walked better, but still with a distinct limp. Instinctively, I learned to walk like a cat. A cat never walks directly into an open room or space, but naturally enters warily, circling the perimeter. And, so did I. Never walking directly toward someone if I could avoid it, but always sliding in from the side, or walking behind someone else. That way I could hopefully avoid the staring. Always, the staring. Walking like that worked so well that later in life people who had known me for years, but never saw the leg, were shocked to find out that I had had polio.

I tried to put my cat-like, peripheral walking to effect at the school dances. As usual, all of the girls would line up on one side of the dance floor, and all of the boys on the other. I found it awkward enough at that age to interact with girls, but the idea of walking directly across the empty dance floor toward the girls was out of the question. Mustering up the grit to ask for one dance was tough enough. I usually got in one or two dances, though, by following another boy across the floor until just in front of the girls.

My dance tactics worked, and left me pleased to be that close to the young ladies. Not only because they were exciting, but also because not once did a girl insult me about my leg to my face, unlike so many boys had done.

Always a big sports fan, one morning during those years I picked up *The San Diego Union* newspaper to read the latest sports news. A local San Diego County boy, Tom Dempsey, had just set the NFL record for the longest field goal ever—63 yards, a great achievement. But in writing the article, the sportswriter highlighted the fact that Dempsey was born without toes on one foot, what was often called a club foot. Instead of featuring his accomplishment, the writer described Dempsey as "the stump-footed kicker."

That outraged me. I could easily imagine how Dempsey might have felt reading the article, knowing all too well what pain those types of insults caused. I mentioned that to Dad, and he encouraged me to write a letter to the paper. I sat down and typed out a letter to the sports editor, the much-admired Jack Murphy. I told him about my own situation, and urged him to publish an apology to Dempsey for such insensitive language by the staffer. I waited in vain for an answer.

CHAPTER 10

MORE SCHOOL DAYS

Helix High School started off very well. Within the first month, my class-mates elected me class president. I enrolled in honors classes, which were not particularly difficult and often very interesting. I signed up for freshman wrestling, which eliminated the agony of regular gym class. Best of all, older brother Glenn, already a junior, gave me a ride to school most mornings, saving me the embarassment of being un-hip and riding a bike.

During Christmas break, the wrestling coaches for all levels of the program held joint workouts. All of the wrestlers practiced together for several days. On the last day, we crowded around the drinking fountain in the locker room after practice ended, eager for a long drink. As I leaned over to take one, a senior wrestler and a star in the program, elbowed me aside and said, "Get out of my way, you crippled idiot."

There again, the C-word. He didn't even know me, had never talked to me, yet he felt free to say that. All I could do was shower and dress, and walk home wondering about the origin of such abject meanness.

High school generally went much better than that. There were few other incidents, and nothing so severe. Besides, my older brother was on the football team, and he and all of his teammates, who liked me, would have beaten the holy hell out of someone who tried it again.

I participated in student government and became very active in Key Club, the service club sponsored by Kiwanis. I did well in class, was one of the editors of the school paper, on the swimming team for a couple of years, and on occasion read the morning school news over the P.A. system. It's fair to say that I was popular, and ran with the in crowd.

My carefree time in school began to change junior year, in 1968. I became much more politically and socially aware of what was happening in the country. I read voraciously, and received mentoring from a teaching assistant in graduate school at the time. He gave me Bernard Fall's *The Two Vietnams* and Arthur Schlesinger's *Vietnam: The Bitter Heritage* to read. Both changed my perception about the Vietnam War, and what the government told Americans about it. I felt estranged from my country for the first time ever.

Glenn and all of his friends were older, and already eligible for the draft. No one wanted to go to Vietnam, and all of them dreaded taking the required physical exam. One of those friends visited our house one day and looked at my leg. "You're so lucky," he blurted out, unprompted. "When you take the physical, they'll declare you 4-F and ineligible to be drafted." I muttered an acknowledgment, but thought to myself "lucky"? I would have traded service in Vietnam for a normal leg in an instant.

America churned with turmoil, highlighted by the presidential election. One spring day, I left school early and drove to downtown San Diego to see Robert F. Kennedy at a large rally for his presidential campaign. I was close to the stage when he spoke, and left mesmerized. A few weeks later, I called his local campaign office and asked if I could volunteer.

That April, the Reverend Dr. Martin Luther King, Jr., died from an assassin's bullet. I had only recently begun to appreciate the man's work, his writings, and his speeches. Kennedy's speech the night of the assassination to an audience on the campaign trail, telling them of King's death and relating it to his own brother's assassination, was brilliant and heart-wrenching. I read the text and saw highlights of it later, and became more determined to support him.

I spent the ensuing weeks thinking about my life, my challenges, and whether in some way I could be involved in public life, maybe make a contribution myself. I thought about Dr. King and the civil rights movement, and had my own moment of enlightenment. If it hurt me so much to be called the C-word, it had to be worse for Blacks to be called the N-word. The word too frequently floated about at school, despite the fact that we only had a few Black students, most of whom I knew. I started asking friends to stop using the word when in my presence. Of course, being snarky teenagers, they began using it even more.

June arrived, the school year coming to a close, and I planned to spend time that summer and fall volunteering with the Kennedy campaign. The night of the California primary, I stayed up late watching the TV coverage of Kennedy winning, and went to bed happy. Mom woke me up very early in the morning to tell me that he had been shot, and that it looked bad. As I drove to school in my old Chevy, the radio came on and said he was dead.

I was scheduled to attend a Key Club International convention in Montreal, Canada, in early July, and I spent the weeks leading up to my departure reading everything I could find about Kennedy. His book, *To Seek a Newer World,* largely a campaign platform piece, already existed. I devoured it, and in particular, his remarks about youth and adventure. How can we deal with evil and suffering in the world? he asked. "Our answer is the world's hope; it is to rely on youth—not a time of life but a state of mind, a temper of the will, a quality of the imagination, a predominance of courage over timidity, of the appetite for adventure over the love of ease."

I learned much later in life that those words were undoubtedly copied almost verbatim from a professor in Alabama, Samuel Ullman. But at the time, I had my direction. I would seek a life of adventure, of challenging myself despite physical limits. I would seek my own newer world, and perhaps do some good in that world. I would be somebody.

With the trip back East that summer already planned, I scheduled an interview with Harvard University. I had decided to apply for admission to Harvard, then considered the number one university in the country. At least I thought it was at the time. The interview went very well, and I walked the beautiful campus afterward, remembering the Robert Browning words that I had learned in school. "A man's reach should exceed his grasp, or what's a heaven for?" Why wouldn't I try to reach the highest rung on the ladder? If Harvard was the best, why not try to aim for the top?

I spent the rest of the summer traveling mostly by myself back across the country. Included were stops at Martha's Vineyard, working on my relatives' farms in the Midwest, multiple national parks, and a week-long national high school journalism conference at Brigham Young University. I arrived home ready for a great senior year.

The year started well. I enjoyed being editorial editor of the school paper, running edgier, more socially conscious work than in the past. I interviewed again with the local Harvard Club, which went well. One member, a local university professor, told me afterward, "Don't worry, you'll get in." A distinguished local alumnus awarded me the Harvard Prize Book, given to the senior boy most exemplary of a Harvard student.

As a gregarious guy, I had many friends at school. One in particular stood out, and in more ways than one. Bill Walton was a year behind me, all nearly-seven feet of him. Bill's older brother, Bruce, was in my class and we were closer. But Bill and I had a strange kind of bond. Bill had a pronounced stutter, which, combined with his young and gangly body, made him clearly self-conscious. I think he intuitively knew that I was self-conscious of mine, too, leading to a warm, unspoken friendship.

Bill was a great high school basketball player, and Bruce a great football player, but I don't think anyone knew at the time how good they would ultimately be. Bruce became an All-American offensive tackle at UCLA, and later played several years for the Dallas Cowboys. Bill became a legendary college and professional basketball star, and an accomplished professional sports announcer.

The friends I had at Helix included many that I knew all the way back in grade school. La Mesa was a very small town atmosphere then, and everyone seemed to know everyone else. Many of those close friends in high school are still close to me today, despite all the intervening years.

Later in the school year, I received several awards. A Bank of America Achievement Award for outstanding college entrance test scores. Co-recipient of the Key Clubber of the Year in California. And, finally, voted Most Likely to Succeed by my classmates. I thought everything was in place for the next step in my life, college.

That step turned out to be a huge stumble. College acceptance and rejection letters came in the mail, and Harvard rejected me. A cursory, thin, two-paragraph letter. Shocked and depressed for days, I couldn't believe that my little dream was over. I didn't know then, and wouldn't realize for several years, but it was the best thing that never happened to me.

CHAPTER 11

WAS GOD MAYBE OUT THERE SOMEWHERE?

Up to that point in life, religion had played only a peripheral role in my life. My parents were believers, and devout enough to go to church every Sunday. My brothers and I attended every week, too, along with Sunday school right after church. We went not because we wanted to, but because we had to. In the summers, we attended "Vacation Bible Camp" for two weeks, which consisted of making lots of little glued-together mosaics of crosses and altars, and being lectured to about Jesus. We wanted to be playing ball with our buddies instead, but we had no choice. We all sang in the church youth choir. In our junior high years, we attended mandatory confirmation classes every Saturday morning. After two years of learning the catechism, we were confirmed into the Lutheran church.

None of it really mattered to me. I don't remember believing, or even praying, except for the ritual recitation of the Lord's Prayer at every church service. I had long since given up on my own little nightly prayer from so many years earlier. It hadn't worked anyway.

Maybe my resistance to organized religion stemmed from growing up in family with a Protestant mother and a formerly Catholic father. Both of my parents were raised on farms in Northern Wisconsin at a time when the two faiths simply didn't intermingle. Dad dropped Catholicism when they married. Because he married out of the faith, not a single member of his large family attended the wedding. Mom must have told and retold that story to my brothers and me a hundred times growing up. Even as children, we understood how asinine that kind of interfaith fighting was.

As soon as high school ended, I started on my "life of adventure," the path that I vowed to take a year earlier. My younger brother Mike and I bought a used fiberglass canoe for $25 and patched it up. We loaded it with gear from an Army surplus store, lashed it to the roof of brother Glenn's car, and headed out. After an all-night drive to the Colorado River, we arrived at dawn. On the Nevada shore, just below Hoover Dam, we assembled our gear, planning to paddle 230 miles down river to Yuma, Arizona.

Glenn had completed the same trip a year or so earlier, which inspired us to try it, too. I also thought it would be a last chance to get a little closer to Mike before I went away to college. Our minature dachshund, Schatzie, couldn't be left behind, so the three of us crammed into the tiny canoe as Glenn drove away. Watching his big Chevy Impala disappear over the horizon, I wondered what in the hell I had talked myself into. It was the middle of August and brutally hot, well over 100 degrees every day of the trip.

On and on we paddled, dawn to dusk every day, stopping only for meals and to rest on shore. We encountered dangerous water conditions, boaters who deliberately tried to swamp us, thunderstorms, and coyotes howling uncomfortably near our camp at night.

For a week, we endured the stupefying heat, sunburn, and exhaustion. After portaging around three dams, we finally approached what we hoped would be our last night of camping. I had a United States Geographical Survey map we followed all the way down the river, so I knew exactly where we were. The map displayed a little general store on the shore, where we hoped to phone home and tell them to pick us up in the morning.

The moment the canoe landed, huge swarms of mosquitoes assaulted us. We tried to march through them toward the building, which was much farther away than the map showed, and looked abandoned anyway. The mosquitoes attacked Schatzie savagely, and we couldn't take them either, so we got back in the canoe and pushed off. It was twilight, darkness coming on, but we had to get away from the insects, into swifter water.

I knew we were in serious trouble. We risked hitting something, or getting caught in fast water and capsizing if we continued on through the dark, but we had no other choice.

Down the river we drifted, squinting into the fading light and hoping for a clean beach where we could camp without mosquitoes. Then Mike shouted, "There, right in front of us, an island!" It was just a small sand bar, but a large miracle. In more than 200 miles of river, it was the only one we encountered. We beached the canoe and quickly made camp in the gathering darkness.

I'd learned during the week that the dams we portaged released water according to irrigation needs downstream, and that river levels rose and fell accordingly. I told Mike we would stay the night unless the river rose. If it did, we would have to pack up quickly and drift all night in the dark, a very dangerous proposition.

Before getting into my sleeping bag, I went to the water's edge and planted our small camp shovel in the sand. If the water started to rise above it, we would leave. Unable to sleep, I listened to the dark river gurgling past us, and stared at the heavenly array of desert stars. I felt so responsible for my younger brother, and also for Schatzie, the love of my life. For the first time in many, many years, I prayed and earnestly meant it. I asked God just to help us make it through the night.

After a long time worrying and staring at the stars, I got up again to check the shovel. The water line hadn't moved, so I crawled back into my sleeping bag and finally fell into a restless sleep. Intending to sleep only a little, I woke up in a panic, not knowing how long I'd been out. At the water's edge, I fell to my knees and stared at the shovel. The river level had fallen several feet below it. I looked up and whispered, "Thank you."

The summer drew to a close, and I began planning for college. The University of California, Santa Barbara, remained my fallback option after my rejection from Harvard, so I prepared to move up there the following month. Mom and I decided to have a last event together by attending a production of the musical *Man of La Mancha*. The same production played Broadway the previous year, and featured many of the original cast members. It was superb.

When the lead actor sang the most famous song from the work, "The Impossible Dream," I melted into my seat. The lyrics hit me like a sledge-hammer: "One man, scorned, and covered with scars, still strove with his last ounce of courage, to reach the unreachable stars." I thought about my own dreams, and still felt like a failure for not achieving them, at least not yet. By God, I swore under my breath, *I would achieve something, someday.* Up to that point in my life, I had rarely expressed much emotion. Maybe all those nights alone in a hospital had hardened my heart, but I was glad that the darkened theater hid from Mom the tears rolling down my cheek.

CHAPTER 12

COLLEGE BEGINS, RELIGION DOESN'T

Life in 1969 at UCSB started on a positive note. The end of high school left me restless, and happy to be away from home. My dorm roommate, Bill, turned out to be a great guy, and still a close friend to this day. Many of the others in the all-male dorm were interesting, fun guys to become acquainted with, too. It was a comfortable place to be, at least until the troubles began.

I naturally participated beyond just classes. My dormmates elected me president of our hall in the dorm. The university chancellor's office asked me to be on a special advisory committee to them. I quarterbacked our hall intramural flag football team, which played well enough to make the playoff rounds. Even though I couldn't really run at all, I could always throw. My leg never came up as an issue, either on the field or back at the dorm.

Studies went well. I didn't find the subjects all that difficult, and enjoyed everything I studied. As the first quarter progressed, though, the campus rumbled with anti-Vietnam War sentiment. Student activists organized mass demonstrations to protect a radical professor the administration wanted to remove. Tension escalated as the war escalated. Rumors of plots to destroy research labs and blow up buildings whipped around the campus like the constant ocean breeze from the waters offshore.

When the quarter ended, I drove home for the holidays and spent a lot of time reflecting. My friends who were also away to college and I compared notes on our experiences. Although happy to be in school and far from home, the thought crept in that I just couldn't stay at that school for four years.

I arrived back on campus in January and began to look at things differently. Despite the beautiful setting on a bluff above the ocean, the whole appearance of the school seemed mediocre to me. The mundane architecture, indifferent landscaping, and general lack of a real collegiate atmosphere left me anxious for a change. The other students were still great to be around, but many of us wondered how the school year would turn out.

I noticed a particular change immediately. One of the two students living across the dorm hall hadn't returned for the quarter. We had nicknamed the missing guy "Sloth," because when he wasn't surfing, he was sleeping or moving languidly. The same radical professor that students protested to protect gave Sloth and two older students nine units of academic credit each to spend the quarter driving a VW van down to surf Central America. All they had to do was write a little paper about their experience when they returned to get the credits. No wonder students protested to keep him on campus. How could I take this school seriously?

As the anti-war protests gathered strength, the mood grew more tense. One night, a raucous crowd gathered in Isla Vista, the student ghetto adjacent to campus. Someone lit a trash dumpster on fire, and while the crowd yelled and chanted, crashed it through the glass doors of a Bank of America branch. Sheriff's deputies in full battle regalia tried to clear a path for firefighters to control the blaze, but to no avail. The entire branch burned to the ground while the crowd and the deputies surged back and forth in a wild melee. Shots were fired, and one student died of a gunshot wound. Sirens wailed all night as tear gas wafted through the campus.

The next morning, I went back to classes. Everything seemed surreal to me, listening to a lecture in my Introduction to Religious Studies class. When the session ended, I pedaled my bike over to the site of the chaos the previous night. I stared at the burned – out hulk of the bank building. The acrid stench of the smoldering rubble still filled the air. I wondered what the point of this had been, besides an anarchistic punch in the nose to a symbol of corporate America. All I could really grasp was that a student had died there the night before, for nothing.

Maybe it was thinking about the meaning of religion, the events on campus, or just general angst; I didn't know for sure. But I began to feel a deep emptiness. Not only wondering what was I doing at this school, but wondering whether my life had a purpose.

I mentioned my feelings to a friend in the dorm, a strong Christian. He suggested I accompany him a few nights later to the campus Christian center.

We went, and the charismatic speaker finished his talk by asking if anyone present wanted to commit their heart to Christ. I didn't understand why, but I raised my hand, and everyone present prayed for me.

One of the fellows down the hall, another devout Christian, heard about my experience and wanted to let me know how excited he was. We were in the communal bathroom, side by side. Me brushing my teeth, and him looking in the mirror when he loudly proclaimed that he wanted to welcome me as a "brother," wrapping me in a hug, despite the toothbrush still hanging from my mouth. I muttered a thanks and looked back at the mirror. "Damn," I said, "a zit." My new "brother" clapped me on the back and said, "Just pray and ask for their removal. It works."

Over the next few weeks, I waited for something to happen. Some sign, some new feeling that would show me my new commitment had substance. I prayed fervently, asking for guidance, for that sign. Eventually, I conceded to myself that nothing had happened, and resigned just to move on.

The main library had a row of catalogues from colleges around the country. I haunted the place between classes, trying to find a compatible fit. I knew I would be applying to transfer somewhere for the next school year, I just didn't know where. Every catalogue appeared to have the same picture of smiling students walking together past classic-looking academic build-ings, with big, leafy trees reflecting dappled sunlight. I didn't care about the similarity of the pictures, just that they looked like a college environment to me.

The campus still seethed with anti-war anger. Demonstration followed demonstration. Sit-ins and class disruptions were an almost a daily occurrence. By spring, the Nixon administration expanded the war effort into Cambodia, and campuses across the country erupted in protest. At Kent State in Ohio, a confrontation between students and the authorities ended in catastrophe when four students were shot to death. Every school in the country raged, and it truly seemed like revolution hovered in the air.

Talk everywhere centered around students organizing a general strike and shutting down campuses. Striking California students would then march on the capitol in Sacramento and shut down the entire state government. After a few days of wild rumor and speculation, Governor Ronald Reagan ordered all University of California campuses closed for a week of "time out."

I decided to use the down time to drive up and see high school friends at Stanford University. When I arrived, the campus stunned me. I had never seen it before, and fell immediately in love. The old stone buildings, the big trees (dappled sunlight), the wide-open setting, and the green, empty hills beyond entranced me. This was where I wanted to be.

Stanford had its own demonstrations going on, but students weren't on strike. Walking across campus that night, we encountered a makeshift stage set up in the courtyard of a building. Students were acting out an improvised anti-war play, *Alice in R.O.T.C. Land*. We watched for a while, enthralled with one especially dramatic student, who gave a magnetic performance. I learned later the aspiring actress was Sigourney Weaver, starting on her road to becoming famous.

I decided on my course of action when I returned to Santa Barbara. Apply to transfer to Stanford or just do nothing, maybe take a sabbatical year off. All that remained was to finish the school year with the best grades possible and go home for the summer, waiting.

Summer flowed along at a mellow, comfortable pace, as summers always did in San Diego. I worked at a very good job as a student intern with the County of San Diego during the day, and partied with friends on the weekends. Every day when I arrived home from work, I first I checked the mail for some word from Stanford. Week after week, no mail for me. I began to prepare for the inevitable disappointment.

One morning while getting ready for work, I received a sign. I didn't know why, but I suddenly knew that day was the day the notice from the school would arrive, good or bad. I called the office and told the secretary who answered that I had a dental emergency and wouldn't be in until that afternoon. It sounded like a plausible excuse to me. Our mail delivery came around noon, so I stayed home and waited, swimming endless laps in our pool to work off the nervous energy.

When I heard the clang of the letter box closing, that sealed it. I walked out to the box, knowing what to look for. A thin envelope: a rejection, a one-page thanks for applying, but no thanks. A fat envelope: admission, with accompanying information. I opened the box, pulled out the mail and just stared at the fat envelope from Stanford, almost too nervous to open it. Life was about to change in a major way.

CHAPTER 13

RELIGION EXAMINED, AGAIN

At Stanford, I immersed myself in the humanities from the first quarter, enrolling in all the philosophy, history, and literature classes I could fit in. The overall atmosphere stimulated me, with great professors and guest speakers, intense impromptu debate sessions with fellow students, and a general intellectual ferment that I loved.

A good friend from high school and I connected right after the year started. He lived in a fraternity near where I was living, so we met frequently. A devout Christian, he introduced me to a number of his fellow Christian students, who happily referred to themselves as "God Squaders." We had many friendly, but sometimes searing arguments about their religion and my lack of one.

They were earnest, sincere, and genuinely nice people, but I found them frankly a bit weird. So self-assured of the truth of their faith that it troubled me. Where was their doubt, their anxiety that maybe, perhaps, they were wrong? Everything I studied led me to more questions. I thought we were all there at that age to question everything. One statement from Socrates learned in a lecture pervaded. "The unexamined life is not worth living."

Classes in philosophy of religion, ancient history, art history, and almost everything else led to questions about my own beliefs and values. Another Socrates maxim, "If there is no God, why be good?" haunted me. Despite all the fun I was having, I couldn't help but think about the meaning of that. My increasing cynicism about religion led me past agnosticism to atheism, a position I thought was the only intellectually defensible one. But, still, what then? Why be good? What was the meaning in life?

I balanced the academics by starting an aggressive fitness program. Several days a week, I rode my bike down to the school's tired old gym building to lift weights. Afterwards, I rode the perimeter of campus to finish my workout. At the gym, I frequently encountered athletes coming in from afternoon practice, including some guys I knew from home. Stanford produced many famous athletes, so it was not uncommon to see someone like Jim Plunkett, on his way to winning the Heisman Trophy that year, or Tom Watson, the soon-to-be golf legend. Inspired by such peers, I was getting into the best shape of my life. Physically, I felt like a normal guy, and mentally, exhilarated by the intellectual environment.

When intramural softball time came around, the semi-defunct fraternity house where I lived as a boarder decided to field a team. I told the organizers that I wanted to play, could hit well, but lacked speed. "Play me where I don't have to run fast," I said, "like first base or catcher."

We had several practices, I did hit well, and looked forward to the games beginning. Then the student picked as captain announced the lineup, and it didn't include me. I confronted him to ask why, and was told something like, well because you can't run, we thought it would be better for you if you weren't out there. Maybe I could pinch-hit sometime. I went back to just exercising on my own instead.

So, there it was once more. The old pity from others I never asked for and certainly didn't want. I realized that it might be there forever. My personal motto had always been the old line about no quarter asked, and none given. Still is.

About that time, someone in one of my literature classes praised Somerset Maugham's work. Curious, I picked up *Of Human Bondage*, maybe his best known work. I enjoyed reading the classic tale of unrequited love, Philip futilely pursuing Mildred, desperate for her attention and love. Philip had a physical condition. Born with a club foot, he limped noticeably and grew up taunted and harassed by his peers. Of course, I identified with him.

At least I enjoyed reading it until late in the novel, when the relationship broke up. Mildred, deciding she now hated Philip, hurls every foul-mouthed invective at him possible. In Maugham's words: "Then she turned around and hurled at him the injury she knew was the only one that really touched him ... she flung it at him as though it were a blow. 'Cripple!' " There was that word again. I put the book down and it really felt like a blow, as if I had been punched in the gut.

My modern philosophy class studied existentialism. To give an oral report on Albert Camus for the class, I read much of what he had written. I couldn't get the imagery of his work, *The Myth of Sisyphus,* out of my mind. Condemned by the gods to push a rock endlessly to the top of a mountain, Sisyphus struggles to understand his fate. As he nears the top, straining as always to push the rock to the summit, it once more slips and rolls back to the bottom. He begins to descend again. At those moments, when he knows what he must do, "He is superior to his fate. He is stronger than his rock," wrote Camus.

One morning I ran late for class and started dressing in a hurry. Without thinking, I stood on my bad leg to put my pants on. I didn't fall over. I stood on the other leg, finished dressing, and then sat down and realized what had happened. I smiled at my reflection in the mirror, enormously pleased with myself. After all those years of trying and failing, I had pushed my own rock to the top of the mountain, where it stayed. It became the first of many mountains I would ascend.

CHAPTER 14

A LIFE OF ADVENTURE—TRAVEL

My junior year of school infected me with a disease. The disease of wander-lust, a condition that has affected me the remainder of my life. At Stanford, like many other universities, we had an overseas program that included our own campuses in various European countries. I chose Germany and spent two academic quarters there.

Eighty of my classmates and I flew over together in the winter of 1972, all of us 19 or 20 years old, soon to be turned loose on an unsuspecting Europe. Although we had full, rigorous academic loads, including some classes entirely in German, we had long weekends and an extended spring break free to travel. Organized group field trips to both Rome and Berlin were part of the cur-riculum, too. Many of us, myself included, bought battered old used cars to roam more freely.

An amazing educational experience, but also an adventure. The adventure of travel, of picking a destination and just striking out for it without reserva-tions or a plan, with nothing but a couple of fellow students, some cheap local wine and cheese, and a map. Of forcing oneself to meet and interact with locals, often in their language. And, I always had along a copy of the legendary *Europe on Five Dollars a Day,* by Arthur Frommer, a sum still possible in those days. In a typically snarky Stanford way, we repeated to each other the phrase, "travel is for those who can't handle the reality of drugs." A funny line back then, even if I never used drugs.

Everywhere we went was special, but one long weekend trip proved particularly memorable. Three other students and I decided to drive my old 1959 Opal Rekord to Zermatt, Switzerland. The car had balding tires and a serious radiator leak, but it worked. One of us wanted to meet up with a classmate from another campus in Italy, but the rest of us just wanted to see the Matterhorn.

We arrived in the dark, and the clouds still obscured the mountains the next morning. My classmate Mark and I set out for a hike up the valley to try to get a view of the Matterhorn. We cleared the village and hiked higher along the trail. Mark, an English major, recited for me snatches of Theodore Roethke poems from his Modern British and American Poetry class. Then, we turned a corner and there it was. I gaped in astonishment at perhaps the most famous mountain in the world. Brutally stark, looming far above us, the morning sun glinting off the rock.

I looked at the sheer face and ragged edges of the peak and wondered how anyone could possibly climb it. I was strangely moved, in a way unlike any feeling in nature I had ever had before. The mountain was calling me to come closer. The semi-hypnotic spell broke when Mark turned and said that we needed to return to the village and meet our fellow students for a drink.

Wandering Europe as a history major made for a magical experience. Studying the history of the continent one day, and seeing the actual sites and buildings the next amounted to pure enchantment. I visited many of the great cathedrals and churches, like St. Peter's and the Sistine Chapel in Rome. Notre Dame in Paris and Mont Saint-Michel in Normandy. The Florence Baptistery, La Sagrada Familia in Barcelona, St. Paul's in London, St. Stephen's in Vienna, and the beautiful ruins of Tintern Abbey in Wales.

Walking through the sepulchral gloom of the otherworldly architecture, the sacred spaces, the light filtering through centuries-old stained glass moved me, but not enough to move my beliefs. The more I examined Christianity, the more I turned away. Nothing about it resonated with me intellectually.

One class did resonate more than others—the philosophy of Friedrich Nietzsche. As I read his work, including sometimes in the original German, it made increasing sense. His scalding critique of Christianity led me to the conclusion that only atheism, and not even agnosticism, could be justified.

Most of the students in our program were paired up with a local family from the little village of Beutelsbach, where we lived. Mine was the Fabriz *familie*, well-known for their warmth and hospitality. *Mutti* and *Vati* Fabriz (Mom and Dad, *auf Deutsch*) welcomed me into their home on an almost daily basis, always with love and open arms. And, then there was Mutti's *apfelkuchen*, constantly available and a local legend.

They were devout Christians, but never pushed it on me. As the months went by, I realized that Mutti's way of expressing her faith manifested in her love for me. She left me a few notes toward the end of our stay, in German because she didn't speak English. She told me of her love for Jesus, and her hope that one day I might open my heart to the possibility of faith. I wondered if she knew something.

When I returned home that summer, I dwelled constantly on the idea of more travel adventures. I remembered my high school vow to live a life of adventure, and now knew that it was possible.

CHAPTER 15

THE NEXT CHAPTER

Senior year back at Stanford went well. The classes, the camaraderie, the parties, the sports teams—I wallowed in everything. I really didn't want to leave, but graduation loomed. Like so many of my peers, I applied to grad school. Everyone, it seemed, planned on either law school or medical school, and a few, business school.

I applied to law schools, and ended up accepted at Georgetown University. I never knew exactly why I applied, but I had a vague sense that a law degree would help me make a meaningful contribution to society. And, Mom and Dad were applying pressure on me to become a lawyer. Not overt pressure, but subtle suggestions that I needed professional credentials.

After graduation, I went home to La Mesa and got a summer job working for the City of San Diego. Georgetown had a semester-based system, meaning a late August start, so all too soon I had to pack up and get ready to head east. A friend from undergraduate days was starting his second year at the school, and flew down from Northern California to drive back to Washington, DC, with me. Off we went, in the middle of August, across the country in my un-air-conditioned little Fiat sedan.

I hated law school almost from the first moment. The pretentious atmosphere, the pomposity of the law professors, and most of all, the vicious competitiveness of fellow students repelled me. Still, I gave it a go for two months. One day I sat in class daydreaming instead of listening to the drone of the professor and asked myself why hadn't I taken a year off before starting grad school. Once the thought entered, I couldn't shake it. Soon, it consumed me—the idea of just dropping out and starting over the next year.

I called the dean of the school and explained my angst. He graciously said, "That's fine, I understand, and we'll see you next year." The packing started the same day.

It took me weeks to make it home, driving across country by myself, stopping to visit friends and relatives in various locales. Most of them asked if I knew what I was doing by dropping out. I always replied that yes, I thought so. Actually, it was an epic amount of time alone to contemplate my life and the future, and I wasn't sure of anything.

By the time I arrived back home, I knew that I would re-apply to law schools for the following year. Not because of a desire to be a lawyer, but because I was never, ever a quitter, and at the moment I felt a little like one. What I would do with the degree once I got it wasn't clear to me, but that was the plan.

I studied up to retake the law school admission test and received very good results. Glenn, recently home after four years in military service he couldn't avoid, and I looked around for a little adventure before starting any jobs. An article in the local paper caught our attention, and we hatched a plan. For the first time in history, Mexico had paved the formerly dirt road all the way down the Baja California peninsula.

In January 1974, just weeks after the road opened, we threw some rudimentary gear into his old Ford van and started south from San Diego, among the first people to ever drive that new road. Camping along the way, the route almost empty, the few people we encountered were friendly and the scenery just spectacular. After reaching La Paz, we loaded the van onto a ferry across the Sea of Cortez to Mazatlán. From there, we drove home through the Sonoran Desert.

After returning, Glenn and I bought an older, ramshackle house as a fixer-upper. We lived among the work clutter for months, planning to sell it to pay for the next school year. Learning renovation skills as we went, the plan worked. We cleared enough profit that I could take off during the summer for a month-long driving and camping trip through the Northwest, including stops to visit law schools that had accepted me.

I focused the trip around various outdoor experiences, including my first whitewater rafting expedition—the Rogue River in Oregon. Tim, a close friend from Stanford, lived near to the river and organized the trip for nine of

THANK GOD I GOT POLIO

us. We had little idea what we were doing, made the descent without guides, and had a genuine adventure. Tim and I led the way down each set of rapids in a rather cheap two-man inflatable raft, paddling furiously through big white-water, then floating the calm waters below. Everywhere, stunningly beautiful landscape. I couldn't wait to try even bigger whitewater on other rivers.

My best friend, Charlie, flew up from San Diego to meet me after the river expedition. We started the trip in Oregon, then moved north to Washington, east to Idaho and Montana, and back to Northern California. Our travels included camping in national and state parks and occasionally staying with friends along the way. By the time my little Fiat made it back to San Diego, I had decided where to attend law school.

CHAPTER 16

LAW SCHOOL REDUX

Of the several schools that accepted me, I chose to enroll at the University of Oregon. To this day, I'm not exactly sure why. Younger brother Mike was finishing up his undergraduate degree there, so I knew a little about the school. The campus seemed small and friendly, the kind of place where I could just get through the experience and then decide on what course life would take next.

Unfortunately, I wasn't any happier in the new school. Although mellower than the Georgetown environment, the school still had a number of jerk students. The kind who always sat in the front row, furiously waving their arms to be called upon by the professor. Law schools attracted that type.

I never found the subject matter particularly hard, just generally boring. I wanted adventure, not legal ventures. After about the third time that someone scratched "Don't Californicate Oregon" into the dust of my car with its California license plates, I admitted to myself the mistake of picking Oregon. I decided to grind it out anyway and at least get credit for the year. By the end of the first semester, I knew I would finish the year and apply to transfer somewhere, anywhere.

The moment the school year ended, in May of 1975, I drove home as fast as I could and caught a flight to Mazatlán, Mexico. There, one of my close friends growing up, Rich, waited with his family's 43-foot sailboat. He and I, along with two other friends from home, planned to sail it back to San Diego.

We paused for several days in the harbor while local mechanics scrambled about, fixing the boat's diesel motor. Finally, we sailed away toward Baja California, across the Sea of Cortez. Leaping sailfish, flying fish bouncing off the waves, and the occasional shark sighting entertained us under the broiling sun. We made landfall at Los Frailes, an almost completely deserted bay, with a long and beautiful white-sand beach.

Mick, another crewman, and I jumped overboard after we anchored and snorkeled our way toward shore. Snorkeling near the rocky heading forming the bay was like swimming in a giant aquarium. We literally pushed schools of inquisitive fish out of the way, while playful sea lions zipped all about.

We sailed the next day down to Cabo San Lucas, then still a rather sleepy fishing village. No condos, mega-resort hotels with golf courses, or wild disco bars. We anchored off the beach for a few days, waiting out a hurricane passing offshore. When the weather looked calmer, we rounded the famous Los Arcos rocks and turned north, with hundreds of miles to go.

From the moment our boat left the protected waters of Cabo San Lucas, the rough-water remnants of the hurricane pounded us. Soon, the prevailing colder wind and swell from the north made foul-weather gear necessary much of the time above deck. We aimed straight into the predominantly north wind, so sailing would have been a far longer and rougher passage. That meant motoring almost all of the way.

With only one small port along our way to refuel, we carried our own extra fuel. The four of us lashed a fifty-gallon steel drum into the boat's cockpit as our reserve, something that left me worried about the chance that it would somehow break loose from the crashing of the boat into the swells.

After two rough days, we finally entered Magdalena Bay. Two nights resting from the strenuous passage and reprovisioning the boat helped. Heading back out to sea near the mouth of the bay, a massive gray whale breached right near the boat, wishing us good luck on the trip home.

Day after day we chugged north, stopping only twice to overnight near offshore islands. We ran all night many nights, which entailed trading off two-hour watches to steer the boat alone. Whoever was steering would tie off the wheel to the cockpit to hold our course, then crawl below to wake the fellow next in line. Strapped into a warm bunk to keep from falling out as the boat lurched about, I did not enjoy putting on foul-weather gear before staggering topside to take over by myself.

We had no radar or GPS navigation system, just the compass to watch as we tried to hold the wheel steady against the pounding sea. More than once, I lost my grip on the wheel and fell backward into the stern rail when we hit a big swell. The boat would stop momentarily, then shudder to life and plow forward.

We motored too far from shore to even see it most nights. When it was there, all was darkness, uninhabited for hundreds of miles. Stars gave the only light. During one lonely, dark turn at the wheel, I recalled John Masefield's poem, "Sea Fever": *"... and all I ask is a tall ship, and a star to steer her by."* All I asked was *get me home.*

Three weeks after I had arrived in Mazatlán, we cruised into San Diego Bay on an overcast June morning. Setting foot on dry land again thrilled me. It had been an adventure, but I vowed never again to take a 1,000-mile voyage on a small boat, into the wind.

That summer, I received notice of acceptance for transfer to the University of San Diego. I could still get my degree in the usual three years and save money by living at my folks' house. They weren't there much in those days; they stayed in the Riverside, California, area most of the time, where they had started a manufacturing business. The place was mine to study in. And, party just a bit, too. I felt so bored with school that I started clerking at a small downtown law firm, both to help pay for tuition and to see if I really wanted to be a lawyer. I went to class every morning, worked every afternoon, and frequently had night classes after that.

In my last year of school, I had a kind of out-of-body experience. One of my professors, Bernard Siegan, had a national reputation of advocating for less government interference in both the law and the economy. As a part of an evening lecture series, the university arranged a public debate between him and John Kenneth Galbraith, the famous economist and author, there to advocate for more government involvement, frankly, in everything.

Siegan, an excellent professor, taught an excellent class. Naturally, I attended the debate. Arriving early to be sure of a seat, I sat in the middle of a row in what became a very crowded auditorium. Next to me were two empty seats, almost the last in the room. Just before the event began, a couple motioned to me from the aisle to ask if those seats were available. I nodded yes, and they sat down. I recognized them immediately. It was Dr. Jonas Salk himself, still working at the Salk Institute in nearby La Jolla, and his famous wife, the artist Francoise Gilot, radiantly beautiful. I looked at them, they smiled and said "Good evening," and I replied the same.

The debate hadn't begun yet, and I sat there stunned. I wanted to reach over past Francoise and shake his hand, introduce myself, thank him for his epic work, maybe even show him my own leg. I hesitated, thinking it might be too rude. Then the program began, and the moment lost. All I could think of later was that of all the people in the world, I sat next to him. I regretted for years not saying something.

Finally, the school year ended and the time to study for the bar exam arrived. Like everyone, I signed up for a seven-week bar review course, listening to lectures every morning and studying in the afternoon. Lectures on the various exam subjects lasted two or three days each. The constitutional law ones extended several days. At the end of that session, I realized that I had just learned more about the subject than I had in a year-long course at school. That depressing realization only confirmed for me what I really thought of the entire law school experience.

A week after finishing the exam, I returned to doing what I wanted to do—off with friends to run a major whitewater river in the Northwest. This time the Snake River through the legendary Hell's Canyon between Idaho and Oregon. Some of the biggest whitewater in the country, the four of us completely on our own for days. I could feel law school fading farther behind with each successive rapid we ran.

CHAPTER 17

THE ADVENTURE OF SPORTS, AND OTHER THINGS

My parents could never tell me why I was given the name Wayne, even though I asked. "We just liked it," they said. I grew up thinking the name odd since it was somewhat rare until one day when I stumbled across an article purporting to describe the origin and meaning of Anglo names. Under Wayne it simply said Teutonic for adventurous. It proved to be true, my whole life.

Moving through college and graduate school years, sports and outdoor activities became more of an obsession than when I was younger. They provided a release from everything else, in addition to being fun. In retrospect, it wasn't just fun, or the camaraderie involved, it was also me trying to prove something. That I could compete, that I belonged, that I was "normal."

My adventurous and independent nature didn't only involve sports. It even preceded polio. When I was three years old, Glenn and I were watching the very popular *Adventures of Superman* TV show. The episode ended and I went outside, where a small rock retaining wall divided the lawn from the driveway. Small, but high to a three-year old. I clambered up it to duplicate what I had just watched Superman do. If he could fly, so could I. I was sure of it. I closed my eyes, and simply jumped off backwards.

I did fly—into a heap on the ground, breaking my arm so severely that the bone stuck out right through the skin. Hearing my screams, Mom ran outside and promptly fainted at the sight. On the way to the hospital, she repeatedly stuffed giant gumdrops into my mouth to stifle the screaming.

At the age of seven, I ran away from home. The morning of the epic day, I had climbed onto the bathroom sink to look into the mirror and examine my teeth brushing effort. By doing that, the sink accidentally ripped from the wall, flinging me to the floor. I told Mom what I did, and she simply said, "Your Dad will deal with this when he gets home."

All day long in school I worried about what punishment I would get when I got home. By afternoon, I hatched a plan. Standing up in class, I announced that I was running away from home, and said my goodbyes.

Back at our house, little brother Mike, then only five, wanted to come along. I wrote a cursory goodbye and you won't see me again note, left it on the kitchen table, and off we went. We marched all the way across town, along with our little dog, Pancho, on the way to the next town where our loving aunt lived. As darkness approached, Mike was tired, so we made camp for the night in a vacant lot. Soon, Mike told me that he was lonely and a little scared, and wanted to go home. I had no choice but to turn back and face the music at home, which was rather severe.

The independent streak always existed. In eighth grade, my social studies class studied the Constitution and how Congress operated. We learned about congressional pages, too, the young men from around the country who actually worked for Congress. They lived together and attended a special school when not on the congressional floor, starting as young as the ninth grade.

To me, that sounded like an exciting opportunity. When I mentioned that to our teacher, Mrs. Stone, she encouraged me to write our local congressman, Bob Wilson, and ask about an appointment to be a page. He graciously replied a few weeks later, thanking me for the inquiry, but indicating that he did not have enough seniority in the system to get me an appointment. The teacher had me read the letter aloud to the class. I felt genuinely disappointed that I couldn't be a page, ready at the age of just 13 to leave home alone and move all the way across the country.

Whatever sport or activity I tried offered its own challenge, exacerbated by my lack of speed and the balance issue of one leg being three inches shorter and far weaker than the other. A leg that has almost no muscle at all below the knee, and little above it.

I gravitated toward tennis, enormously popular during college years in the early '70s. After a tennis class, a couple of more lessons and a lot of practice, I became modestly proficient, within my limits. I could serve well and hit a forehand, but when it came time to shift my weight to the other side for a backhand or run to the net, weak at best. Still, since so many friends played, a doubles game was always available. In doubles, I could cover my assignment. I played for years, but eventually lost interest. I knew I would never get any better than my own level of averageness, and I moved on.

I took up skiing in college, too. For my first trip, I went to a ski shop near campus, rented gear they told me would work, and drove with friends to Lake Tahoe. The friends were brilliant skiers, so I signed up for a lesson by myself and thought, how hard can this be?

The lesson turned out to be completely useless. Standing on uneven ground next to the instructor, I struggled to get the skis on, and once I did, had no idea how to stop myself from sliding backward into the parking lot. The instructor laughed, offered little advice, and after a few more minutes, I said just show me how to catch the bunny slope chair lift and leave me alone.

The instructor never even showed me the most basic of maneuvers, the snow plow, to control speed or to stop. Getting off the chair lift for me that day meant just falling to stop. Over and over again, all day long, I collapsed in a heap, then struggled to my feet and attempted getting down the gentle slope.

It was a small ski resort, and there were very few on the bunny run. The same little girl and her personal instructor went by me all day long. After another, inevitable fall on the slope, I struggled in the snow trying to get up when the girl passed overhead on the ski lift. She shouted down to me, "Can I ask you a question?" I looked up at her and answered something like yeah, sure. "Ok," she chirped, "are you having fun?"

I made two more ski trips with friends that school year. Excellent skiers, they gave me useful instruction, like setting ski edges to turn and control speed, then left me to practice. I made endless traverse runs across the slopes, able to transfer my weight and turn on the good leg, and then when I got to the other side of the slope, turning on my weaker leg proved almost impossible. Usually, I just planted my poles to try to stop, or just fell, got up, and aimed the other direction.

Eventually, I bought my own ski boots, which helped somewhat. I learned to link up a few stem turns and make it down intermediate slopes. While I beat the hell out of my body trying to get better, at least I had fun being with my skiing friends.

Like every physical endeavor I attempted, the challenge of proving myself drove me. My breakthrough came years later when I discovered an incredible ski shop, Footloose, in Mammoth Lakes, California. I went in to have my old boots tweaked, but instead, accepted their expert advice and bought new, high-tech ones. They completely tore apart the boot for my weaker leg and heavily customized it to compensate for the weakness. One of the owners, Corty Lawrence, took a personal interest in my situation and spent hours during several trips to the store making the boot right. He knew a little about skiing. His mother, Andrea Mead Lawrence, won two gold medals in downhill skiing for the U.S. in the 1952 Winter Olympics. He even introduced me to her one day when she was in the store and I was in the fitting chair.

The boots made an almost miraculous difference on the slopes. I realized that I could transfer weight from one leg to the other like anyone else from the very first run. I skied properly parallel and went down harder slopes. Within days, I was a skier.

Golf is another sport requiring balance and an ability to properly shift weight from one side to the other to make shots. I started playing in law school, learning to compensate somewhat, but never played very well. Despite playing frequently, I arrived at my own plateau of mediocrity.

By the early '90s, my bad leg began to collapse on me at the end of a long work day. The hyperextending backward caused me to consult with an orthopedic surgeon, who recommended that I see prosthetic specialists. They convinced me to try an AFO, or ankle foot orthotic. Essentially, a custom-molded, plastic leg brace from the knee all the way down. It locked the ankle like a ski boot and made walking very awkward at first. But I have worn one every day since, and couldn't live without the stability it gives me. Abandoning my steel braces as a little boy was one of the great days of my life, making it odd to reflect on the fact that I willingly accepted one again.

With the brace, I had to learn to swing a golf club all over again. I hit endless practice balls, ultimately becoming comfortable with the new reality. My game improved to the point that I could consistently shoot in the 80s. I play infrequently now because of other ailments, but I did have the privilege of playing such renowned courses as Turnberry, St. Andrews, and Gleneagles in Scotland, and Pebble Beach and Torrey Pines at home.

My best golf memory came not when I was playing, but as a spectator. In 1997, a friend whose family had lifetime passes to the Masters Tournament in Augusta, Georgia, invited me to attend. We had a terrific time absorbing the exceptional experience of just being there. Additionally, one player made history that year by destroying the field and winning his first major tournament by a record margin. I naturally rooted for him anyway as a fellow Stanford guy, but it was a stunning performance to witness in person. His name—Tiger Woods.

San Diego practically invented racquetball. In the early years of the game, everyone played and I did, too. For many years, I played on almost a weekly basis, becoming pretty good. The court was small, so I didn't need big speed, just quickness.

Rich, my friend from the long Mexican boat ride, told me about a bike race that he had entered and said why didn't I come along. I think he meant come along to drive one of the support vans, but I said sure, why not? I intended to ride. I hadn't ridden a bike since college, and in fact, didn't even own one. A few days before the scheduled ride, I went down to a local department store and bought the cheapest imported ten-speed I could find.

The ride was the Tecate to Ensenada, Mexico, race, with thousands of entrants. Seventy-seven miles through mountains and hills, and I did nothing to prepare. I heard second-hand that a friend, an NFL football player, told some of our mutual friends that I had no chance to finish the race. That provided the kind of motivation that drove me all of my life, so I knew I would make it.

The store didn't tune the new bike properly, and the gears began malfunctioning a few miles in. I ended up stuck in higher gears most of the way, but finished. Near the back of the pack, but finished. A few years later, on a better bike and after many preparation rides, I rode again and finished in the top 10 percent of all riders. I was comfortable enough during the ride the enjoy the scenery through the Valle de Guadalupe. Now, it's a world-class culinary and winery destination.

During those years, I frequently connected with college friends when they were in town. One afternoon, two friends who also lived in town called to say another couple we knew were visiting, and would I like to join everyone for dinner? All of us had been together in Germany, so we were having a fun evening, sharing memories of that wonderful time. I told one story that made us all laugh, and the visiting fellow said, "You know, Wayne, you're a funny guy. You talk funny, and you walk funny." That gratuitous remark came from one of the smartest students I met at school. I didn't bother to dignify it with a response. When the couple from town called to apologize profusely the next morning, I simply told them to forget it, and that I never liked that bastard anyway.

CHAPTER 18

MORE ADVENTUROUS SPORTS

I loved the challenge of participating in sports, competing, pushing, trying to prove myself. But always present was a lingering sense that I needed something more, an element of risk, even danger. I tried many different endeavors, and some provided the kind of exhilarating high I craved. Where that craving came from, I wasn't sure. Maybe a desire to show myself and the world that a child considered sickly and weak could one day overcome anything.

Near the end of my high school years, Glenn returned from what he told the family was a camping trip to the Sierra mountains. It turned out that he had climbed Mt. Whitney, the highest peak in the continental U.S. at 14,495 feet. That sounded like a great challenge. Especially when Mom, hearing of the climb, turned to me in her excitement and blurted out, "Now that is something you'll never be able to do." She immediately apologized, and mumbled that she shouldn't have said it because it would only encourage me. I just replied, "You're right." A few years later, Glenn and I decided to climb the peak.

We were young and vigorous, so we just grabbed some old camping gear and set out, with no training or preparation. We arrived at the Whitney Portal base in the dark, and tried to sleep in my miniature Fiat. At first light, the climb began.

It was a very long, 21-mile slog, not technically difficult, but not easy, either. We had the gear with us, but instead of camping along the way, just pushed on to the summit. I wished that I could see the magnificent view from there, but the clouds moved in and obscured everything. Bitter cold enveloped us, so we signed the book in the climbers' hut and hurried back down the mountain.

We rested where our gear was stashed. Glenn made soup to warm us up, and after the nourishment and a few shots of the alcohol we brought along to celebrate, I felt pretty good. Exhausted, but good.

A brilliant full moon started to rise over the darkened granitic rocks of the canyon, lighting up the trail with reflected light to the point that we could clearly see the path. Glenn asked if I thought I could make it. "Let's try," I said. We descended almost to the car before stopping for a little sleep. My leg screamed at me all the way down, but it was worth it. I had camped, hiked, and backpacked in the mountains many times before. This was different. I summited my first mountain and felt ecstatic. Actually, I had summited Mt. Lassen in Lassen National Park years earlier, but that was a much shorter and easier route, really just a long hike.

Whitewater rafting always appealed to me. The beauty of the wilderness, carrying everything with us in the raft, camping alone on a remote river beach—all magical. The real appeal, though, was the challenge, even danger, of the rapids. Together with college friends, I ran some of the biggest whitewater in the country, including the Rogue, Illinois, and Deschutes rivers in Oregon, and the Snake through Hell's Canyon in Idaho and Oregon.

We never used guides, doing everything ourselves, from planning the logistics to learning to scout the water and of course, navigate the rapids. It added to the challenge and adventure.

Heights never frightened me. In fact, I enjoyed them. I liked looking down from the edge of a cliff or the top of a high-rise building. Not surprisingly, flying thrilled me. I took a couple of flying lessons, but didn't pursue a pilot's license. I did fly many times with friends in their small planes and couldn't get enough of it.

The ultimate small-plane experience to me was jumping out of one. I signed up for a one-day class, went through the practice drills on the ground, and off we flew. There is nothing quite like crawling out on the wing of a plane, looking down several thousand feet, the jumpmaster yells, "go!" and then just shoving off. Perhaps the only thing more exhilarating was looking up as I dropped away and seeing my chute deploy above me. Not sure if there could be a better feeling in the world.

Scuba diving intrigued me from my earliest years. I earned my certification to dive in junior high school, but didn't do much with it in those days. My friends and I did a lot of snorkeling and spear-fishing after that, but no scuba.

Years later, I took up scuba again when I started traveling to exotic locations. I enjoyed thrilling moments while diving in many of the best spots in the world. I dove the Great Barrier Reef, Thailand, Baja California, Santa Catalina, Belize, Honduras, the Cayman Islands, the Bahamas, Turks and Caicos, and Turkey. I still hear the siren call of many other remote destinations, too, and hope to dive again soon.

CHAPTER 19

THE ADVENTURE OF TRAVEL

Nothing in my life to that point, however adventurous, excited me as much travel, or the anticipation of travel. It was as if the travel bug that I contracted after returning from school in Europe possessed me. Instinctively, I agreed wth Mark Twain. "Twenty years from now you will be more disappointed by the things you didn't do than by the ones you did do. So throw off the bowlines. Sail away from the safe harbor. Catch the trade winds in your sails. Explore. Dream. Discover."

Finishing undergraduate and graduate school took precedence before I could head overseas again, but I began to plan. New Zealand intrigued me in particular. Everything about the country seemed exotic, from the very name to the fact that it was so far away, and that no one I knew had ever visited there.

I saved enough money by law clerking before and after the bar exam to afford a trip. In 1977, a few weeks after the test, I flew down under. That was long ago, long before the economic revolution that revitalized the country. Their stagnant economy at the time left the country bordering on poor, giving it the air of a time warp. I thought that I had somehow returned to the 1930s or '40s. And the allure of Old England fused with the native Polynesian Maori culture made an enchanting combination.

As quaintly charming as everything appeared, the outdoor adventure possibilities really energized me. I traveled the entire country by hitchhiking, rental car, buses, ferries, small planes, and even their tiny, narrow-gauged railway. Everywhere I went presented another opportunity for an outdoor experience.

I skied Mt. Ruapehu, a still potentially active volcano, where signs warned skiers that, "In the event of an eruption, please move to higher ground." That amused me, thinking of myself in ski gear trying to escape by going up, not down. In the distance, another old volcano, Mt. Ngauruhoe, still had smoke wafting from its volcanic center.

I flew in a small ski plane to the top of the Tasman Glacier, where the guide led us, skis on our backs, on a climb higher up to the top of the ridge. There, the incredible view led all the way down to the Tasman Sea, with other glaciers visible in all directions. The wild and rugged terrain had served many years earlier as a training ground for Sir Edmund Hillary, the native New Zealander, before his historic first ascent of Mt. Everest.

We skied down carefully, warned by the guide to follow his exact tracks to avoid disappearing into a crevasse. Twenty-two miles later, the little plane picked us up at the bottom of the glacier. After the pilot took off, he flew directly toward the base of Mt. Cook, the highest peak in Australasia. He wanted to show us the mountain up closer, and as he did, a large avalanche tumbled down the mountainside directly in front of us.

I hiked the Franz Joseph and Fox glaciers, floated through the absolute darkness of glow worm caves, and fly fished the world-famous Tongariro River (with absolutely no luck). I visited the awe-inspiring fjords of Doubtful Sound and Milford Sound, and stayed at one of the best-known sheep stations in the country, Glendhu. At Glendhu, going on "muster" to find sheep on the isolated, 20,000-acre station felt like I was literally at the end of the earth. The novelist Samuel Butler wrote his novel, *Erehwon*, nowhere spelled backward, after a long stay at a similar station not far from there.

The most exciting thing I did happened with a group of young fellow travelers that I met along the trail. They were from Australia and Canada, and we traveled together for days on the South Island, pausing at Queenstown. Among Queenstown's many attractions was the nearby Shotover River, famous for shallow-draft jet boats escorting loads of tourists through swift rapids.

As an old gold mining area from the nineteenth century, rusted, abandoned mining equipment littered the river's edge and the steep canyon walls. We drove our rental car along the river, stopping to inspect some of the old gear and take pictures. Then, we discovered a flying fox.

A flying fox was a kind of wooden seat attached by chains to a pulley cable system. In earlier days, the seat provided the only way to cross the churning rapids of the river, handlining with the pulley to the other side. One of the Australians jiggled the rusted lock and chain around the seat, and it literally came apart in his hands. We looked at each other and agreed to do something crazy.

I volunteered to go first, not knowing how many years or decades it had been since someone had used it, or, more importantly, whether the cables would hold my weight over the roaring river. I jumped in, the guys gave me a starting push, and I shot out over the Shotover. It was thrilling to still be in the seat swinging above the rapids mid-river, but much more so to have the pulley cables hold up as I hauled myself back to shore.

After the group split up for a few days, we reassembled in Christchurch. From there, the two Canadians, twin brothers Mark and Peter, and I hitch-hiked north to Kaikoura. In the native Maori language, Kaikoura means "feast of crayfish." Crayfish, or lobster, were harvested in the beautiful little fishing town nestled between the Pacific and a snow-capped mountain range just beyond.

A hostel for accommodations sat right on the water's edge and next to a small fresh-fish market. The only other guests were a young American couple. All of us went together to the market to buy just harvested crustaceans for our own "feast of lobster."

Everyone prepared the delicious meal in the hostel kitchen. The American couple talked about taking a sabbatical year off from their teaching jobs to travel around the world. They were just beginning, with New Zealand the first stop. Mark and Peter were actually doing the same thing, just starting their round-the-world year, too. I listened wistfully to their plans, looked with them at maps they had brought, and all I wanted to do was to be them. To be on my own round-the-world trip. When I returned home, I immediately began planning that trip, the ultimate adventure.

CHAPTER 20

THE ADVENTURE OF TRAVEL, AMPLIFIED

I worked for the next year and a half as outside counsel to the small manufacturing business Dad had formed. The work wasn't exciting or fulfilling, but I felt like I was helping out.

Living very frugally, I managed to save a fair sum of money for my trip. I read whatever I could find about backpacking through various countries, and planned where I would travel. Very little specific material existed in those days, though. Fortunately, a couple of young ladies in town had just finished a similar trip, and they happily shared extensive travel tips over a couple of bottles of wine.

By January 1979, the time finally arrived to commit. I bought a new traveler's backpack and a one-way ticket to Australia, via Fiji and Hawaii. I had a friend getting married in Hawaii, and a friend in Sydney I stayed in touch with after we had met a few years earlier skiing in Utah. That was the extent of the preplanning. No reservations, no other flights booked, no schedule or timetable other than the goal of traveling overland whenever possible, using local means wherever I could.

The plan was to start by seeing as much of Australia as possible, then fly to Bali and start moving overland through Southeast Asia and on to India. I eagerly anticipated duplicating the path of the historic Grand Trunk Road, New Delhi to Istanbul, all the way on the ground. But, just weeks before I started, the Iranian revolution erupted and the government of the Shah fell. "Death to America" immediately became the cry in Iran, meaning it would be extremely dangerous to travel across the country as a solo American backpacker. I decided I would worry about that decision months later when I got nearer.

Australia offered one adventure after another. Scuba diving on the Great Barrier Reef and body surfing at Bondi Beach. Hiking in the rain forest with clouds of budgies flying overhead and pademelons, a small relative of the kangaroo, running through the dense undergrowth. I encountered koalas, fairy penguins, wombats, kangaroos, giant cane toads, fruit bats, and kookaburras, all in their natural wild habitats.

I hitchhiked, took local trains, buses, and some flights to get from one end of the enormous country to the other. Then, Asia called. I boarded a flight in Perth and arrived in Bali on a steamy tropical night. My first night ever in Asia. Perfumed air permeated everything.

Bali then was nothing like the trendy, ultra-hip getaway for wealthy tourists and surfers it later became. Fellow backpackers comprised most of the visitors, and the whole island had an aura of calm serenity. Meals and lodging were ridiculously cheap. The ancient local culture, the warm people, and the scenery mesmerized me.

When I wandered through crumbling temples covered in vines, packs of wild monkeys followed everywhere and parrots squawked overhead. The smell of grilled satay skewers wafted through the air as locals went about their daily lives, largely ignoring us tourists. They tended rice paddies, cared for temples, and occasionally marched past in colorful funeral processions.

I usually spent the end of a day sitting on the beach, watching the sunset with other travelers. A cold $1 Bintang beer in hand and maybe a $2 massage on a mat on the sand. Then off to a local cultural performance, like Balinese dancing or a gamelan orchestra.

A couple of fellow travelers and I pooled our money to rent a Jeep. We drove to the other side of the island, visiting temples along the way. Somewhere up in the verdant volcanic mountains, with no one else around, we stopped the Jeep when we noticed a figure walking up the hill toward us. It was a beautiful Balinese woman, wearing sandals and the customary wrap-around skirt, and nothing else. One arm was stretched up to balance the large basket of fruit on her head. Topless, in the traditional way, moving with the same quiet grace as centuries of Balinese women before her. She flowed past without making eye contact, leaving us speechless at her beauty.

The time to begin the trek across Asia came. A series of local jitneys carried me over the island to a little port. I caught a leaky old ferry across the

Balinese Strait to a small town with the big name of Banyuwangi and headed west into Java.

The decrepit local vans would only go so far before a mandatory transfer to another one at the next town or village. They were stiflingly hot, packed with locals and sometimes their animals. I crammed into one after another all day long, the only Westerner, communicating by sign language and the little bit of pidgin Indonesian I had picked up. In those days, few people in rural Java spoke English. Out the open windows, I watched men and women escape the intense tropical heat by splashing in the rivers we passed by. They were usually naked, despite it being a Muslim country, and eagerly waved to us.

After two days, I arrived in Jogyakarta, the center of Javanese culture and arts. The cultural scene was remarkable, but everything paled in comparison to Borobudur, just outside of town. The largest Buddhist temple/ruin in the world, Borobudur survived from a time centuries before the country converted to Islam. The faithful covered the entire surface in bas relief carvings of the Buddhist story. Worshippers would read the carvings as they ascended the spiraling, long walk up to the top, where a massive ancient volcano loomed in the distance. I marveled at the religious fervor that created the monumental work. As a non-believer then, I could appreciate the effort, but couldn't understand the fervor.

Back in Jogya, as locals called it, I ran into a solo traveler I had seen in Bali. We decided to travel together to Jakarta. That pattern repeated often over the coming months on the "Overland" route, striking up a conversation with another backpacker in one of the cafes or bars where travelers gathered, linking up to travel together temporarily. Sometimes for security reasons, but usually to combat the loneliness of going around the world by oneself. Since most of us were traveling on the ultra-cheap, also to split the cost of a ride or a room.

We took the all-night train to Jakarta, an ancient steam locomotive, the type of working relic that railroad buffs traveled the world to watch operate. Except that this one was the only train on the main railroad line. It broke down suddenly in the middle of the inky-black night for a couple of hours, but we eventually arrived in the city in the morning.

Morning in Jakarta revealed an awful place—crowded, polluted, steaming hot, and not particularly friendly. We did see one scintillating sight, though, the Pasar Ikan, Indonesian for fish market. The old waterfront packed with working wooden sailing ships, still the merchant fleet of Indonesia. They sailed to all of the hundreds of islands in their archipelago, one of the last fleets like that in the world. Reputedly, many of the vessels were actually pirate ships, too. We hired a local with a rowboat for a few Indonesian ringgit and took a ride between the vessels, wondering which of the hostile-looking sailors staring at us might indeed be pirates.

I flew across the Java Sea to Singapore from Jakarta and planned to travel north into Southeast Asia using local, land-based transportation wherever possible. I wanted to experience the world, not fly over it.

Singapore was evolving from the British colonial era, with many modern buildings surrounding an old urban core still intact from the nineteenth century. The city offered an intoxicating mix of cultures, races, languages, and food. The food stalls in old Chinatown alone were enough to cause a swoon. Wafting saffron and curry from Indian dishes, Malay spices, the scent of Thai lemon grass and kaffir limes, next to crackling Chinese noodle bowls. After a generous sampling, I made my way to the Raffles Hotel bar for Singapore Slings, where they were invented. Later, I took the aerial tram out to Sentosa Island to visit the extensive parks.

The next night, a visit to the infamous "Boogie Street." Boogie Street, a derivative of the actual street name, Bugis Street, served a dual purpose. A parking lot by day, but at night, proprietors cleared out the cars and filled the space with tables and chairs. A full bar and food stalls were rolled out, and tourists filled the tables as the sun set and the oppressive equatorial heat began to dissipate. The evening wore on and a lively crowd enjoyed more drinks. Then, a sudden buzz filled the air when they appeared.

"They" were the infamous Asian "Lady Boys," young men in high heels, slit-skirted dresses, and impeccable make-up, gliding silently between the tables. They moved languorously, the tropical heat adding to their sultriness. All gorgeous, and with their fine Asian features and slight bodies, almost impossible to distinguish from women. Two heavily-drinking Australians at the next table admitted to me that one of them had been fooled the night before, taking a Lady Boy back to his hotel room, only to discover that the lady was indeed a boy.

After a few days, I went to the main train station early in the morning and bought a ticket north. The train clattered along all day through lush green fields and hills until we reached Kuala Lumpur, the capital of Malaysia. After a day sightseeing there, back on the train to Penang and Georgetown. I met more travelers while touring around, including a pair of young English women who were also doing the Overland route, only in the opposite direction, across Asia from west to east.

Over drinks that night in a local foreigners' bar, they told me of crossing from Turkey into Iran. The revolution in the country raged, the Shah exiled abroad, and the Ayatollah in power. They described a place seething with hatred, especially of Westerners, and in particular, of Americans. They urged me not to go. Listening to their stories, I became convinced that if I followed my original plan and took local buses through Iran as they had, I would be in serious danger. But, my decision could wait until I got to India.

Before I left the Penang area, I visited the famous Bayan Lepas snake temple. Nearly two hundred years old and architecturally beautiful, the real attraction slithered everywhere. Green pit vipers, highly venomous and not defanged, crawled on almost every surface. Legend had it that the overpowering incense burning inside the temple calmed them into not biting. For a small donation, a monk brought one to me. Quite a sensation to have something that dangerous sliding up my arm and around my neck. Not as dangerous as the Ayatollah might be, I thought.

The train carried me to Bangkok and the confusing congestion of one of the most vibrant cities in Asia. Smells filled the air from the ubiquitous food stalls, the rotting leftovers in the streets, and the flowering trees. Honking, horrendous traffic, beautiful ancient temples and palaces, and masses of tourists. Everything made an indelible impression.

I had always planned to stop for a while in Bangkok to rest up and organize the next legs of my odyssey. I got my shots updated, went to various embassies for visas, and visited "bucket shops." Those were small travel stores located anywhere tourists gathered, all selling incredibly cheap flights, seemingly from every airline in the world. Since I had to fly to get to Burma, and from there to India, I shopped hard for the best deal. (It was Burma in those days, not Myanmar, and always will be to me. I have used the same names of the places I visited as they were back then throughout the book). I booked the Burmese national carrier for my first segment, which proved to be rather problematic.

When the day came to catch my flight to Rangoon, I went to the gate they announced and stood around with the small number of other passengers taking the same flight. We waited, and waited longer. Then, they announced a mechanical problem, "soon to be fixed." We waited a while longer. Finally, an airline representative gathered us together to reveal that it was a navigational problem, and since the flight would be in the dark, they would get it fixed by the morning and put us all up in a local hotel for the night.

We landed in Rangoon the next day, and I paused on the way out of the plane to talk to one of the pilots, a Westerner. I told him that I was glad they got the problem fixed, and he replied that they never did. I was incredulous. He laughed and said, "It's Burma." He explained that in the daylight, they could just navigate into Rangoon by looking for the sun reflecting off of the golden dome of the massive Shwedagon Pagoda towering over the city. Welcome to Burma.

The autocratic Burmese government had reopened the country to tourism only a few years earlier, after being a closed society for decades. It was primitive travel, with almost no tourism infrastructure. Tourists were allowed just one week in the country, strictly enforced, and all financial transactions had to be accounted for in writing to ensure that no black-market currency exchanges occurred. I promptly ignored the law, selling the bottle of Johnny Walker Red and carton of cigarettes I brought along for that reason in a back-alley transaction, giving me enough extra Burmese currency to enjoy myself a little.

I met other travelers on the flight, and together we bought tickets for the all-night train to Mandalay. To see such a large country in just one week, we had to move quickly. After a tour of the magnificent Shwedagon Pagoda, we boarded the train for a miserable night of sitting upright the whole way in a brightly lit, very uncomfortable car. The only relief was an austere cafe car, which closed a few hours into the trip.

Mandalay was a dusty, crumbling, ancient place, somnambulant along the Irrawaddy River. I walked among the old temples and ruins, with snatches of Rudyard Kipling poems flashing through my head. Then we all booked a local plane to Pagan, the only way to get to that stunning place.

When we boarded the carrier, Union of Burma Airways, I looked around at the poorly maintained, dirty plane. For the first time in my travels, but not the last, a thought came to me. I was traveling completely alone. What if the worst happened? No one in the world knew where I was at that moment. How would anyone find out? I dismissed the thought until the engines roared to life and an overhead panel fell off onto my head. Had I been a believer then, I would have prayed fervently.

Pagan had a remarkable history. A thousand years ago, a flourishing city stood there, containing hundreds of thousands of people. Genghis Khan and the Mongol empire ruled central Asia then, their tentacles extending in all directions. According to one apocryphal story, the Pagan court treated an emissary from the Mongols rudely. That enraged the Mongol emperor, and he sent his army south. They obliterated the population of the city, leaving Pagan empty, to brood alone for centuries in the tropical sun and monsoonal rain.

There were once more than four thousand temples and pagodas in Pagan, and many still stood, vacant and forlorn. I wandered among them on a wooden cart pulled by a tired old pony, with no other tourists around, lost in the ethereal beauty.

We gathered that evening back at our very spartan accommodations to share a meal at the one "restaurant" open. The menu offered some sort of stew and little else. Half way through the meal, one companion traveler, an Australian veterinarian, picked at the bones in his stew. "We've been eating cat," he announced. Welcome to Burma, indeed.

Back in Rangoon, we had one last wet night to savor the country. Not because of weather, but because the impoverished Burmese had little to celebrate other than their Thingyan New Year festival. Part of the traditional celebration included pouring water on each other, a kind of happy purification ritual that signaled washing away the sins and problems of the previous year. Smiling, laughing locals walked up repeatedly and threw glasses of water at us as we just tried to eat at a small outdoor cafe.

I had a mostly sleepless night in the hostel that passed for a hotel, frequently awakened by gigantic insects crawling on me. We all left in the dark to walk to the old Strand Hotel, bastion of the British Empire back in the day. The Strand served as a central location to catch a bus to the airport. As we walked there over the broken sidewalks, what were surely the largest rats in the world scampered in front of us.

The flight to Calcutta, India, gave me time to reflect on my trip to that point. Overall, I was immensely pleased. There had certainly been negative moments and experiences, but those were far outweighed by positive ones.

I gazed out the window at the Andaman Sea below and idly wondered what drove me to make the trip. It definitely wasn't to prove anything to anyone. No one I met out there even knew that I had ever had polio. It wasn't to find myself spritually, since I didn't believe in God at the time. And, it wasn't to run away from anything, either.

I traveled to run toward something. Toward that life of adventure I vowed to myself years earlier. As a young boy, I loved history, geography, and studying maps. Reading about foreign places enthralled me, and here I was, experiencing them in person. The same boy who had once been told he might never walk again was wandering alone through the world. I felt as alive as anytime in my life, determined to see that world.

CHAPTER 21

THE ADVENTURE OF EXOTIC

Landing in Calcutta overwhelmed me immediately with the chaos and crush of humanity everywhere. A Canadian couple that I met on the plane and I shared a taxi into the heart of the city and found a very cheap, but very clean hotel. After Burma, it seemed downright luxurious.

We took human-powered rickshaws, which still existed then, to the Medan central park and toured the stately old Victoria Museum. The colonial history exhibits and the collection of Mogul miniature paintings were impressive. We saw the site of the infamous "Black Hole of Calcutta." After an eighteenth century battle, over 100 captured British troops were imprisoned there in a tiny dungeon. They all suffocated to death in just one night.

Then we decided on something a little more unusual. The Howrah slums across the river were said to be the worst in the world, but I needed to see for myself. It was where Mother Theresa operated her famous orphanage. We negotiated with a taxi driver to take us there and back, a relatively simple proposition.

As soon as we crossed the bridge over the Howrah River, the driver refused to go into the area, claiming it wasn't safe. He stopped the taxi while we argued with him. Soon, we were surrounded by a large group of locals, all crowding into the open windows of the cab. One asked, "Excuse me sir, what is the problem here?" I explained that we simply wanted to see their community, and that the driver wouldn't honor our agreement. All of the others began shouting at the driver, who finally relented and drove us through the streets. Although impoverished, Howrah had a true neighborhood feel, and I was glad that I experienced it.

From Calcutta, I flew into Kathmandu, Nepal. The flight alone made for an adventure. The short runway gave little margin for error, and the pilot slammed on the brakes as we skidded to a stop at the very end, buildings looming up directly in front of us.

The whole Kathmandu valley had an enchanting, ancient air. The mostly wooden buildings, elaborately carved with sacred and profane decorations, were centuries old. Twisted cobblestone streets wound up and down hills crammed with those wooden buildings. Each street dotted with little restaurants, many catering to backpackers, trekkers, and mountain climbers. Above the valley loomed the Swayambhunath temple, with gigantic eyes of Buddha painted on all four sides, because Buddha sees all. Monkeys—considered sacred—scrambled everywhere. They knew they were protected, and would steal anything you left unguarded.

As usual, I linked up with other travelers I met along the way. Together, we planned a mini-trek to the Annapurna range of the Himalayas. That involved an all-day local bus ride to Pokhara, in the western part of the country. Jammed into a rickety bus, luggage riding on top with the animals, we wound our way over dangerously narrow mountain roads, which clung to precipitous canyon walls.

After a day of acclimation, we started hiking along a trail carved by centuries of Nepali farmers and traders carrying their goods over the highest mountains in the world to Tibet. "*Namaste*" to everyone we encountered on the trail. At the end of the day, we reached a little house operating as a travelers' rest stop. The minimal charge to stay included a bowl of desperately needed rice dahl and sharing our chocolate bars with the resident children, who never stopped smiling. We stayed in an upstairs loft along with a half-dozen other trekkers, and tried to sleep on a hard, mat-covered floor.

The view the next morning made a very uncomfortable night worth it. The prevailing daytime haze that obscured the Himalayas during those months of the year had dissipated by morning. Directly behind us loomed awe-inspiring Machapuchare, known as the "Fish Tail." Nearly 23,000 feet high, sacred to Nepalis, the mountain to this day has never been summited. So clear in the dawn light that I felt like I could reach out and touch it. Decades earlier, the King of Nepal declared that the god Shiva lived at the top of the mountain and forbade anyone from ever climbing to the top.

Back in Kathmandu, I booked a special Royal Nepal Airlines flight that featured a slow fly-by of Mt. Everest. From the air, we could clearly see the Khumbu icefall, the sister peaks of Lhotse and Nuptse, and a spectacular Mt. Everest.

After Nepal, I flew back to India and the holy city of Varanasi. I booked a predawn tour, which began at the shore of the sacred Ganges river. The first shafts of sunlight illuminated the ghats, ancient steps down to the river and the funeral pyres waiting to be lit. Soon, families of the deceased would light the wood stacked under the bodies, then, ultimately, scatter the ashes into the holy water of the Ganges.

Our small wooden boat chugged back and forth past the ghats, many of the steps filled with devotees bathing in the river, while nearly naked Sadhus, holy men, sat motionless beside them. As I looked at the activity on the ghats, something floated past us. It was a body in rigor mortis, sewed inside a burlap bag. Perched on the face was a large raven, plucking out the eyeballs. Individuals not considered pure at death were not allowed to have their ashes spread in the holy river, so the whole body would be dumped. Nothing quite like seeing all of that before even a first cup of coffee.

The boat tied up at a dock, and we climbed up the ghats, past the burning funeral pyres and into the narrow warren of paths through the old town. We squeezed our way past the crowds, vendors crying out to us to look at their wares. Then, someone grabbed me from the side. I turned to look at the hand clutching me, and much of it was missing. I stared at the face of a withered old woman, most of her nose gone. A leper, begging.

It was such a shock to have her touching me that all I could do was hand her a couple of rupees and hurry to catch my group, trying to remember whether leprosy was contagious. Scrambling through the crowded alleys, I couldn't get the image of the old woman out of my mind. I knew too well what agony it was to endure constant staring. How much worse must her life have been?

The next destination was Agra, home of the Taj Mahal. I arrived near dusk, but the grounds were still open. Almost no one was there, so as I passed through the entrance archway, the unimpeded view simply took my breath away. I gasped when I saw the most beautiful building in the world, the fading light reflecting off of the semiprecious stones set in translucent marble walls.

I went back very early the next morning with two other travelers from the hotel I stayed in, splitting a hired car for the day. Too early for other tourists, so we didn't have to share the magnificence with anyone. After many photographs, our driver took us south to Fatephur Sikri, a literal ghost town. Laid out as a planned city by brilliant Mogul architects around the time the Taj Mahal was built, it was to be the capitol of the Mogul empire in India.

They planned for everything, except an adequate water supply. Abandoned after just a few years, Fatephur stands there alone today, beautifully preserved after hundreds of years. While we wandered the deserted central courtyard, a turbaned old man played a mournful tune on his ancient instrument, enticing a hooded cobra to rise up out of the basket in front of him.

On the way back to Agra, we stopped in the empty countryside to witness a bizarre sight. Alone on the side of the road stood a man, waving at us. Except, he wasn't entirely alone. He had a dancing bear on a leash, a sad-looking, tired old beast. The man was waiting for someone like us to stop and give him a rupee or two to make the bear spin around. Reluctantly, I gave him one, hoping he might buy the bear a meal. India had an inexhaustible supply of exotic sights.

I caught the evening train from Agra to New Delhi, pulled by an old, coal-burning locomotive. Passengers crammed in everywhere, and all of the windows in the car were open because of the stifling heat. Without my knowing it, coal dust from the engine blackened the side of my face and hair. When we arrived in New Delhi, people were staring at me. I didn't know why until I finally got to a hotel-room mirror.

I saw all the sights in New Delhi with my new friend, Davies. We first met in Burma, then traveled together in Nepal, and planned a rendezvous in New Delhi. I did a little shopping for supplies, and battled a nasty case of "Delhi belly." After months of street food and unusual local cuisine, my digestive system was in full revolt.

The Iranian revolution loomed as a major problem. By then I knew I couldn't safely cross through the country, so a journey through Pakistan and Afghanistan would require doubling back to India to fly west. The U.S. embassy had to have more information on conditions in those countries, so I dropped in and immediately saw a sign asking Americans to please stay out of Kabul, Afghanistan. It warned of unsafe conditions and stated that if you encountered trouble, there was likely nothing they could do to help.

Not much choice but to linger in New Delhi and take the ultra-cheap flight I bought in Bangkok on to Frankfurt. There, I would visit friends in Germany and begin working my way east to make up for missing the Overland route from Asia. I planned to travel southeast to Turkey, then head back west and return home.

CHAPTER 22

EUROPE AGAIN AND HOME

When I landed in Europe, seven years after finishing school there, everything seemed familiar. After the heat, dust, and chaos of Asia, though, a bit of a shock. Everything clean, almost antiseptic, and so mild in temperature. Within days, my German language skills returned. I felt comfortable wherever I went in Germany, visiting friends and seeing many famous sites that I had missed the first time in the country.

One place in particular I had to visit again was the little village, Beutelsbach, home of our Stanford campus. I had sent postcards from Asia to my German family, not knowing whether they were ever received, or whether they knew at all that I planned to visit at some point. After hitchiking my way through the countryside, I boarded a short train to Beutelsbach.

Departing the small station, I found a pay phone and called "home." Vati answered and told me in German that, indeed, they knew I was coming, just not when. He assured me that they were ready for me, and asked, *"Erinnerst du dich an den Weg?" "Selbstverständlich,"* I told him. Of course I remembered the way. After stumbling somewhat lost through the village streets, I finally found their street and began walking up the hill with my bags. When I reached the top, there he was, smoking his constant cigar, patiently waiting in the middle of the street in front of their house. Mutti waited at the front door, with open arms. I felt as though I had never left. After being alone for so long, to experience their enveloping love and warmth again was just magic. And, Mutti had made *apfelkuchen*, as always.

I wallowed in nostalgia a couple of days longer before leaving the village, then began the trip toward the east. Whatever cheap train rides I could find,

I booked. Down through Munich, sightseeing in Bavaria, and on to Austria, visiting areas I hadn't seen the first time in Europe.

After lingering a while in the Alps, another train ride south to Italy, heading for Venice.

Venice was new to me. I had visited Italy several times before, but never Venice. Even back then, tourists jammed the narrow walkways, restaurants, and *vaporetto* boats serving as taxis on the water.

Finding a room for the night proved difficult. A fruitless search produced nothing but, "sorry, no vacancy," in Italian. I sat down and contemplated taking the night train somewhere, just to sleep on it. Then I ran into a young Canadian woman and her mother traveling together who had been on the same train from Austria that morning. They experienced a similar lack of luck finding something affordable. The three of us, total strangers, decided to pool our money to get the only room we could afford.

Wandering through the back alleys and absorbing the history and romance of the incredible place captivated me. I stopped to enjoy a snack of *piccoli morsi* and a local beer, trying to avoid the crush of tourists. Eventually, I found my way to the famous Harry's Bar, planning to have a drink to honor Ernest Hemingway at one of his favorite bars. The host took one look at my months-long beard and rumpled travel clothes and almost didn't seat me. I explained that I only wanted a Bellini, their legendary drink that Hemingway loved. It was actually the only thing I could afford, and even that, just barely. Afterward, I went outside into the Piazza San Marco and sat alone for a while, thinking.

I realized how tired I felt after so many months of almost constant travel. I certainly realized that my money had just about run out and that I was beginning to use a credit card carried only for emergencies. My plan had been to take a train to Trieste, on the Yugoslavian border, and from there catch a cheap Yugoslavian state ferry, which ran all the way down the Dalmatian coast to Greece.

There still existed a chance to make a scheduled rendezvous in Athens with a buddy from home. The more I thought about travel, though, the more the exhaustion crept in. A gondola slowly moved past between the piazza and the little island of San Giorgio Maggiore. Sitting near the Bridge of Sighs, I sighed with a little disappointment myself. Venice, or *La Serenissima*, the

"Most Serene" as the ancient moniker goes, worked her magic. I decided that it was time to go home, and felt serenely comfortable with the decision.

I went to the train station the next morning and began catching trains across northern Italy, then up through Switzerland. There were new places to see that I missed the first time I visited, so Switzerland proved a great spot to wind down the journey. Then a train back to Frankfurt and the flight home.

Arriving back in San Diego very late at night, I took a cab from the airport home, literally using the last few dollars left. I rang the doorbell and Dad came to the door, not knowing who it was at such a late hour. I shouted through the door, "Will you give a weary traveler a bed tonight?" They were thrilled to see me, and me them. It was good to be home. Minus 30 pounds and one tooth that went bad during the trip, but with a lifetime of memories.

CHAPTER 23

BACK TO WORK, RELUCTANTLY

I started working for the family company again to get back on my feet financially. Dad had a tentative deal to sell the whole operation to a large customer and needed my help negotiating the details. Interesting for a while, but all I really wanted to do was to continue traveling. Make enough money to begin another months-long journey, this time down through Mexico to South America.

We consummated the deal after a few months, providing me a little income to buy a small condo as an investment. I settled into the condo life and soon realized that things were becoming a bit too comfortable. The South American trip called, but in the interim, some buddies and I put together a trip in June of 1980 to the East Coast and the Caribbean. We were having a great time until I got a late-night call from Dad. He told me that the purchasing company had sued on allegations of financial irregularities. Since the buyer was a Fortune 500 company suing for more than 10 times the purchase amount, I knew we were in for a horrendous battle.

For most of the next year, I worked with the counsel we hired, constructing our defense. Ultimately, we forced the case into arbitration, instead of a courthouse, but that didn't mean any less work. It was a boring, emotionally draining grind. In the end, the arbitrator readjusted the purchase price in their favor somewhat, but given what we had faced, the outcome was essentially a draw, minus all the enormous legal fees. I felt as if I had just lost an entire year of my life, for nothing.

The whole experience soured me on the legal profession. Nauseating claims by opposing attorneys, claims based on erroneous conclusions or simply false information, will do that. Unfortunately, it was not going to be my last awful experience with litigation. Years later, an even worse case haunted the family, one so horrible that it led me to question everything, including what little faith I had.

CHAPTER 24

ALMOST TOO MUCH ADVENTURE

One day during the grind of litigation, a friend I met originally while traveling in New Zealand came to town to visit. Mike lived part-time in Thailand and had started dealing in gemstones on a small scale. Investment-grade gems were very popular then, and Thailand was both a source of sapphires and an important trading center. It sounded very intriguing, so we made a pact to partner up, borrow some serious money, and see if we could make real profits. Of course, it also meant another adventure in Asia.

I met him in Bangkok, and we began visiting all the gem-trader contacts that he had made. Clearly, deals were available for high-quality stones. We waited to begin buying until we had more information, and booked the all-night train to Chiang Mai.

Mike lived in a rental house in Chiang Mai, in the cooler, greener, far north of the country. It was near the border with Burma and on smuggling routes. Burmese rubies were the best in the world, and frequently brought across the border at nearby Chiang Rai. We thought of heading there, but it had been shelled over the border by the rebel army of General Kuhn Sa a few months earlier. He was at war with the Burmese government, and had been for decades. We decided to let the stones come to us in Chiang Mai.

Through word of mouth, a young Burmese smuggler showed up with some nice gems. I bought several and asked him if he could return quickly with more. Actually, I asked through Mike, who spoke very good Thai. The smuggler spoke Thai, too, as a product of the border. He smiled and replied that nothing was that easy.

Mike owned an old jeep, a great way to roar around Chiang Mai. One day we drove with a Thai friend of his, a working tour guide, to see the ethnic hill tribes in the Golden Triangle. At the time, that border of Thailand, Laos, and Burma was the prime source of opium in the world. After visiting a tribal village, we received permission to travel higher up to their working fields, permission rarely ever granted. I walked alone through the opium poppies, some of the flowers slashed to cause their narcotic ooze to begin flowing. A hill tribesman shouldering an ancient but working rifle watched me warily the whole time.

Drugs created a strange dichotomy in the country then. Use and possession were completely illegal, but I was in one of the major producing areas of the world. The next day, the reality of the subject intruded in a shattering way. Mike had been asked to give a talk to a group of American students starting a semester abroad at the local Thai college, to describe expatriate life in Thailand. I accompanied him to listen to his presentation.

After Mike spoke, the next speaker was the resident U.S. consul general, there to beg the students not to get involved with drugs. He told them that just the day before, local Thai police arrested a young American traveler in his hotel room with a fortune in drugs in his bags. The consul said that there was really nothing they could do except to console the traveler's family, because he faced decades in a Thai prison.

Driving through Chiang Mai the next afternoon, we encountered a major traffic blockage. Locals told us that it was a kidnapping or robbery hostage situation. We saw a vehicle surrounded by police with guns drawn and later learned that a Thai thug had taken hostage the wife of the local U.S. Drug Enforcement Agency representative. He held a pistol to her head in the car. After a stand-off lasting hours, the gun went off, killing her. The official account in the English-language papers in the morning said that the criminal had no idea who she was and never meant it to end that way. The tropical heat in the car caused his sweaty hand to slip, the account said. We learned the truth later.

Mike's friend, Bill, lived outside of town in the countryside. We visited him that night, driving out in the darkness in the open-topped jeep. Bill served during the Vietnam War with the C.I.A. in Laos, working with Hmong fighters. He stayed on after the war as an ex-pat, living in the Chiang Mai area for years. Fluent in multiple languages, including Thai, he told us what locals were already saying about the incident. The shooter definitely knew who the victim was, and her connection to anti-drug efforts. He added that word was out for Americans to lay low. When it came time to leave, he retrieved his service pistol, a loaded .45 caliber, from a drawer and told us that he would provide cover. He stood in his darkened doorway as we walked out to the jeep, trying to appear calm. Nothing happened, but I didn't exhale until we arrived back at Mike's rented house.

We finished in Chiang Mai, needing to get back to Bangkok to buy more gemstones. The all-night bus offered an affordable option, so we booked it. Hours into the trip, somewhere in the middle of a forest on the dark highway, I had almost fallen asleep out of exhaustion when a loud crash startled everyone awake. The bus lurched wildly right and left, then accelerated as the driver desperately tried to avoid a makeshift roadblock set up by robbers.

The crash was the sound of something thrown at the windows, one of which shattered near me. Once safely far enough away, the driver turned the bus lights on, and the attendant gasped when she saw me. Blood dripped down my forehead from a cut caused by the shattered glass. She murmured something sweetly in Thai, and handed me a Band-Aid.

Back in Bangkok, we scurried among gem traders, buying the best collection we could afford. After assembling the stones, I needed a place to stay with an impregnable safe. I rewarded myself by booking my last night at the Oriental Hotel, then ranked as perhaps the top hotel in the world. I sipped one last Singapore Sling on the patio overlooking the Chao Phraya River at sunset, watching the parade of long-tailed boats roar past. The bejeweled Wat Arun temple across the river winked at me when the fading sun glinted off its side.

I stopped at Hong Kong, Macau, and Hawaii on the way home, in part to show the stones to a couple of dealers, and because those locations were along the way back.

I wore a passport pouch everywhere I went, containing tens of thousands of dollars worth of gemstones tucked under my pants. It gave me an odd feeling, at once exciting, yet frightening.

While in Hong Kong, I booked a quick trip into Shenzhen, the People's Republic of China. That was only a few years after China allowed travel for Americans again. We took a train to the frontier border, walked in past glowering Chinese guards, and boarded a bus for a tour of the little village. Smiling locals in Mao jackets, their normal dress, greeted us everywhere. Today, that same little village is a massive city of high-rise buildings, and a center of Chinese commerce.

Ultimately, we sold the jewels for a very nice profit, but the market had already softened for collectibles. After attending a couple of large national gem shows, I decided there really wasn't a future in that business. Despite that conclusion, I knew how much I had enjoyed the excitement and even danger of the venture. Almost anything was more exciting to me than the dull grind of working as a lawyer.

CHAPTER 25

THE ADVENTURE OF LOVE

Not long after I returned home to San Diego, I sold my condo for a small gain and rented a modest, one-bedroom apartment at Mission Bay. The unit sat right on the water of the bay in a small building where friends already occupied a place. It had a mostly private beach, palm trees, a hedonistic atmosphere, and even a nickname—"Peyton Place Under the Palms." The residents were all still young, or young at heart, and we enjoyed a lot of fun. A *lot* of fun.

Although I dated frequently, I had honestly never been in an extended relationship in my entire life. I had carried the proverbial torch for a couple of women years earlier, but the interest never seemed reciprocal. Friends joked that my average dating relationship lasted approximately two and a half weeks. That wasn't far off. I just never happened to meet anyone that I wanted to spend extended time with and began to assume at 33 that I would be a happy bachelor forever.

Then, I met Kaye when a mutual friend introduced us. We connected immediately, beginning what for me was a long-term relationship. She had a special combination of beauty and intelligence, combined with a wonderful, funny personality. I never dated anyone else again.

Eventually, I gave up my beloved beach apartment and moved in with her. I had never been so compatible with someone before. A few months passed, and I realized that it was marry Kaye, or I would probably never marry. When I finally asked her, she replied in her usual laconic fashion, "Well, we seem to get along."

For all of her marvelous qualities, though, Kaye had a serious defect. She had a cat. I think she loved cats more than people. Henry was a big, orange tabby happily ensconced when I arrived, and seemed to like me. I didn't like him, because as I explained to Kaye, I grew up violently allergic to cats. Hated them. I finally told her that Henry had to go.

When she heard that, Kaye paused thoughtfully for perhaps a second or two, and simply said, "Henry was here first." I immediately looked for Henry to ask if he wanted a treat or two. By living with a cat for the first time, my childhood allergy, which had already dissipated, faded altogether. I grew to love Henry, and all the subsequent cats we've had, even when they try to sleep near my face.

We thought of getting married in a foreign country, but quickly realized that would be unaffordable. We settled on Santa Fe, New Mexico, instead, about as close to foreign as you can get in America. In March 1985, a number of friends joined us a week early in Taos for skiing, then 50 family members and friends gathered in Santa Fe for the ceremony.

The morning of the wedding, I wandered alone through the historic town square, trying to rehearse out loud what I planned to say at the wedding dinner that night. She meant so much to me, and I kept choking up with emotion. When the time came for my toast to her, I told the group that the moment had been a long time coming, and that I had assumed I would just be a bachelor all my life. I added the following: For a long time, I agreed with the writer H.L. Mencken, who said, "If I ever marry, it will be on sudden impulse, as when a man shoots himself." But then I met Kaye. Now I agree with Shakespeare, who wrote, " When I said I would die a bachelor, I did not think I should live till I had seen your face." (I paraphrased Shakespeare just a little bit.)

She was the first woman I truly felt comfortable standing in front of naked, meaning not covering up my deformed leg. I knew she accepted me for who I was, not how I appeared. Like any long-term relationship, we have certainly had our ups and downs, but after several decades of marriage, she is still my best friend in the world. That, I think, is the ultimate test of love.

CHAPTER 26

AT THE MOUNTAIN OF MADNESS

The year after our wedding, Kaye and I started planning our first overseas trip together, a kind of delayed honeymoon. We settled on England and Scotland, and planned a marvelous itinerary. But before that, I had a side trip to make. Our new family business had contracted with an entrepreneur to manufacture a part for snow skis that he designed. The part was a prototype, to be incorporated into skis made by a famous Austrian ski company. With Europe already scheduled, I decided to travel early to Austria and deliver the parts personally.

Once I booked Austria, I started planning another side trip. I had just finished a book called *The Adventurer's Guide*, by Jack Wheeler. The author wrote a whole section on climbing the Matterhorn, including some how-to tips. Kaye thought me seriously mad to even think about climbing it and told me so, but an obsession overtook me. I was in excellent shape, and working out constantly. I thought I might just be able to do it, but shared the idea with no one except her. Frankly, if I failed, I didn't want others to know. We arranged to meet in London after my attempt.

A few months later, I visited the ski factory outside Salzburg, Austria, delivered the parts, and then reserved the overnight train to Switzerland. I arrived in Zermatt the next afternoon and immediately looked for the *Burgführer Verein* office, headquarters of the mountain guides. Because of the book, I knew to ask for Alfons Franzen, one of the best-known senior guides, and famous in his own right. Years earlier, he had been featured in the Disney movie *Third Man on the Mountain*. I was in luck—Alfons was available to guide me.

Alfons and I talked about the logistics of the climb, and what I needed to do to prepare. First, he directed me to spend the next day hiking the trails above the village to acclimate my legs and lungs. The following day, a climb up to the practice mountain, the Riffelhorn, where we would drill on techniques, including rappelling and crampon use. Only if I did well enough that day, and only if he didn't think that I was a risk to both of us, would he lead me on the Matterhorn.

We finished the conversation on the cobblestone street outside the *Verein* office. As I walked away, he noticed my limp and called after me. Was something wrong, he asked. No, I said, I'm fine. Knowing the question was coming, I added, *"Nicht in den Beinen, Sondern im Herzen."* It's not in the legs, but in the heart, in German. He understood, and gave me a kind of wry smile.

I took the route he told me to the next day, hiking far above the village. A beautifully clear morning, with the Matterhorn looming across the valley. I reflected back to that day in college when I first saw it. Again, the same odd sensation overcame me. The mountain spoke to me once more, calling me closer.

I finished my day of hiking solo and reported to his house the next morning. The views from the top of the Riffelhorn were spectacular, especially of the Matterhorn. When we descended, he shook my hand and said congratulations, you have just climbed your first peak in the Alps. Then he stunned me with the news that we were starting our climb of the Matterhorn that very night. He said that we needed to take advantage of a weather window, and had to start right away.

Alfons told me to go back to the hotel, gather my gear, and meet him that night at the Hornli Hut at the base of the mountain. Climbers spent the night before their summit attempts in the Hornli Hut, at 10,578 feet. I hustled back to collect things, caught the last funicular train up from the village to the Schwarzsee stop, and began hiking up to the hut. I had a bite of dinner, chatted with other climbers, and then Alfons arrived. He showed me my bunk, and told me to have everything laid out and ready to go in the early morning darkness because we would be the first climbers out.

Up to that point, I had been too active to feel anxious about the climb. But in the dark and silent hut later, I couldn't sleep. Doubt began to overtake me. What if my leg gave out? What if I fell? My leg was already rubbery from days of hiking. Lying there, I remembered that day with my classmate, Mark, years before. Mark reciting Theodore Roethke poetry as we hiked toward the Matterhorn. I studied Roethke myself the next year on campus, and his lines flowed back to me: "I learned not to fear infinity, the far field, the windy cliffs of forever," from his poem "The Far Field." That calmed me. What did I have to fear for trying? No one in the world except Kaye even knew of my attempt.

I must have slept a little, because before I knew it, Alfons woke me to say, "Hurry, Wayne, one cup of coffee and we leave." We began climbing in total darkness, hours before sunrise. Alfons wanted his clients to feel the climb holds, so he wouldn't allow gloves. In the dark, I cut my hands repeatedly on the sharp and crumbling rock of the mountain. A fellow climber told me later that night over beers in the village that when it became first light, he just followed my bloody trail.

We climbed for hours, roped together. Alfons above, with me following, placing my hands and feet exactly where he did. We never paused until first light. He allowed me some water, an energy bar, and a few moments to savor the most beautiful sunrise of my life. All around me, massive alpine peaks glowed pink in the slanted morning light. Everything just stunning, and I couldn't wait to climb higher to see more.

Once it was light, the drop-off from either side of the ridge we were climbing became clear. I didn't have time to look down and worry, because I had to keep up with a human billy goat. From where we crossed the last ridge to the top, it's a sheer, 4,000-foot fall down the slope. I never thought about it, though. I couldn't. I focused on following the guide, one foot after the other, until the summit.

A team of very experienced Japanese climbers actually caught up to us just before the summit, but otherwise, we were the first ones on top. At nearly 15,000 feet, the view is so spectacular that mere words don't do it justice. Even now, I can close my eyes and see that view in detail, like an unforgettable movie scene. To the west, Mont Blanc, 100 miles away. Below me to the south, all of Italy spread out as far as I could see. In the other direction, so far below it looked like a child's tiny play set, Zermatt, surrounded by Monte Rosa and other peaks. All of it brilliantly clear in the morning light.

We couldn't linger. Alfons wanted to head down before the sun began to loosen the packed snow and ice on the route, making our crampons useless.

And, before other climbers still ascending plugged the narrow, dangerous route. We made good time descending, my leg getting weaker and weaker, roped to Alfons above, belaying me at risky spots. I worried that the leg would give out and willed it forward with every ounce of energy that I had.

A tiny emergency hut existed about half way down, where we paused to catch our breath and drink water. He said he could see that my leg was giving me trouble. So, I did what I almost never did. I pulled up my pants to show him the withered leg. He shook his head slightly and said, "Had I known that, I wouldn't have taken you." I explained to him what had happened, and then asked how I had done. He smiled and said, "You did very well." That, from a man like him, was enough for me.

I went to his house that evening to pay him his guiding fee and return the crampons. Then I walked, or rather staggered with cramping legs and bandaged hands, to the beautiful little cemetery in town. There were the graves of many of the climbers who died on the mountain over the years since it was first climbed, lying under crossed climbing axes. To this day, climbers die trying the Matterhorn almost every year.

I silently congratulated myself that I had made it. I should have dropped to my knees in prayerful thanks, but I still wasn't a believer, other than in myself. It hadn't been just an adventure. It was an attempt to prove something, not only to me, but to others and I did.

CHAPTER 27

HIGHER AND HIGHER

Back home, life returned to normal, but only for a few months. Kaye and I had talked about a safari to Africa to see the wildlife before it all disappeared, and began loosely planning a trip. Unrelated to the planning, I heard a radio ad for a charity event one afternoon while driving around town. The group holding it asked the public to donate for a climb up the stairs of a downtown high-rise building. For every step up, contributors were encouraged to sponsor a certain amount. That seemed like an interesting way to raise money.

A few days later, a thought teased me. If we were really going to Africa, why not combine a safari with a climb of the largest mountain on the continent, Mt. Kilimanjaro? Of course, I had no idea how to start that kind of planning. We had always been members of the San Diego Zoological Society, and it sponsored member tours of Africa. I contacted the tour operator to talk about possibilities. He assured me that combining the climb and a safari wouldn't be a problem, and that he could arrange both.

We pored over articles about Africa, building ideas for the trip. I read everything I could find about climbing Kilimanjaro and started to ramp up conditioning, knowing it would be a very strenuous endeavor for me. Our excitement grew with each new article or idea.

Then another thought came to me, this one a kind of epiphany. There I was, healthy, happy, and planning the trip of a lifetime, but something was missing. I realized that after so many years, I had never thanked the people at Children's Hospital for what they did for me. Once the idea entered my mind, it took hold like a fixation.

How to properly thank them? The answer finally occurred to me, and seemed obvious once I thought of it. I would climb Kilimanjaro as a benefit for Children's Hospital, in effect telling the world how it had helped me. Just like the local charity event that I had heard about on the radio, I would ask for donations for every step I took. I settled on one penny for every foot of Kilimanjaro's 19,340-foot elevation.

A friend worked for the hospital's charitable foundation, so I asked her for help. She facilitated a meeting with the heads of the foundation to allow me to pitch the idea. We agreed on a time to meet and a place, at their temporary trailer. Children's was beginning a major building program, and many of the personnel were housed in trailers.

I had not been back to the hospital in many, many years and promptly got lost driving around looking for the right trailer. Back and forth I circled until, after another wrong turn, I arrived at the old brick front entrance to the hospital, which I recognized from so many visits as a boy. I was not just lost, but very frustrated. The hell with it, I thought, maybe this idea just wasn't meant to be.

At that very moment, the front doors of the hospital opened, and there she was. She staggered straight toward me—a little girl about four years old in a pink dress, struggling with her crutches and braces. The same age as I was when I went in the first time. She looked right at me, with a smile. I was about to leap out of the car to help her when several adults emerged to assist her back through the doors. I turned the car around, found the trailer, and swore that I would not let her down.

After I made my proposal, the two executives paused, and asked me one question. Did I think that I could make it to the summit? I understood their skepticism, and then told them about the Matterhorn. That sealed the deal. They brought in more staffers and we began to plan the campaign of fundraising and publicity.

I worked out furiously, before work, after work, weekends, whenever I could hit the roads on my bike or work the rowing machine I had bought. I started drafting the fundraising letter I would send out to family and friends to ask for donations. It was 1987, still before the digital age, so everything was done what is now considered the old-fashioned way.

My birthday fell during that time. Several friends came over for dinner, and everyone brought a birthday card, as usual. One couple's card stunned me. Inside was a joke cartoon about a one-legged man. As I stood there, a look of shock might have crossed my face because they said to me, "Now don't get upset. It's funny. It's just a card."

It had been many years since something like that happened to me. Later that night, when everyone was gone, I couldn't help but think that I would never really escape my fate. If I needed more motivation to make it to the top, I had just received it.

One day, the fundraising team from the foundation asked me to come to the hospital to speak to a large group of doctors and nurses and tell them why I was doing the climb. Although a very polished public speaker during my career, I had never spoken in public about my experience with polio and Children's, and rarely in private. Still, I thought it would be an easy conversation and was eager to oblige.

At the end of my brief remarks, I began to tell them about having never thanked Children's. I looked out at the room full of professionals working to save children every day and became so choked up that I couldn't speak. I grabbed for what I thought was a cup of water near me, but it was steaming hot coffee. Later, I walked back alone to my car with a slightly burned throat and the realization of how much repressed emotion was welling up in me.

Back home, I took time to revise and polish the fundraising solicitation letter before it went out. I started by describing those first days of contracting polio, and why I was now doing the climb. I mentioned the penny-for-every-foot-climbed contribution, and concluded with these lines from Ernest Hemingway's "The Snows of Kilimanjaro": "There, ahead, all he could see, as wide as all the world, great, high, and unbelievably white in the sun, was the square top of Kilimanjaro. And then he knew that there was where he was going." I ended by simply asking, "Come with me—for Children's."

It had an almost immediate impact. Soon, checks to Children's arrived at our house almost daily. We carefully recorded every name, to be later carried by me to the summit.

As the fundraising began, the Children's public relations folks cranked up their outreach. They were very effective. They featured me in their widely distributed magazine, *Children's News*, in a piece entitled, "San Diego Adventurer Climbs Kilimanjaro For Children's." Articles about me and the climb appeared in all of the local newspapers. Many of the local radio stations did live interviews, and almost every TV station did a special segment on my effort. Some stations even did a second story as my departure date got closer.

Meanwhile, the checks kept coming, most with a personal note. For a traditional mail solicitation, we were doing very well. The personal notes were often heartbreaking, frequently from parents of other Children's patients who had learned of the quest. Many of those patients had had life-threatening illnesses, and some didn't survive.

One note in particular moved me like no other. I sat with Kaye in the kitchen, going through that day's mail when I noticed that one envelope came from a good friend of hers. I opened it, and along with the check, her friend included a small picture of a very young boy. The boy was clearly disabled. The accompanying note said it was of her younger brother, born with spina bifida. She said that as he grew older, he grew increasingly bitter. "I hope that some of your courage will rub off on him," she wrote. I handed the note to Kaye to read and began sobbing. I understood for the first time that my endeavor had become much bigger than just me, and that my life indeed had a purpose.

One of my final public relations appearances occurred two days before we departed. A popular local morning TV show, *Sun-up San Diego*, asked me to appear live in studio to hand all of the checks to the chairman of the Children's board of trustees. A great moment that generated even more checks.

Mom called me the day before we left. She was crying and terribly worried about me. I told her, "Mom, don't worry, because I'm on a mission from God." After we hung up, I reflected for a moment, thinking that maybe it wasn't just a glib phrase. Maybe something more was happening.

CHAPTER 28

POLE, POLE

The morning we departed, the head of fundraising for the Children's Foundation surprised me at the airport gate with a Children's balloon and a special T-shirt they made up for me, highlighting the climb. We boarded, and as we were taking our seats, a flight attendant approached. I thought she wanted the balloon, but she asked me to de-plane. Back at the gate, a local television anchor and his cameraman were there to interview me one last time.

Once airborne, I realized how exhausted I was, physically from training and mentally from the whole endeavor, including the many publicity events. A 36-hour trip to our destination of Arusha, Tanzania, completed the exhaustion. But, if there is anything to restore one's energy and excitement, it's beginning an African safari.

We lucked out right away when another couple who were scheduled to share our vehicle cancelled. That left just Kaye and me and our Tanzanian driver/guide for a full week safari in a four-wheel drive Volkswagen van with a pop-up roof for photography. A private safari through the major game parks of northern Tanzania. The vehicle even came with a small, built-in refrigerator, so I had cold Tusker beer always available.

We loved everything during the week. Very few other travelers, but incredible numbers of animals and stunning African scenery. Then back to Arusha for a last night, where we met another couple from California who had also booked the Kilimanjaro climb with the same travel agent. In the morning, we were all driven to the airport to drop off Kaye, who was flying to Europe to wait for me until after the climb.

Saying goodbye at the airport was difficult. I assured Kaye that I would be fine, but I knew there was always risk on any mountain. Just a few months earlier, a young American woman had died of a pulmonary edema while attempting the same climb.

The other couple, Diane and Jerry, and I arrived that afternoon at the Mt. Kibo Hotel. All of the climbers who were also on that week's trek assembled the first night for a briefing by the trek organizers. They introduced us to our Tanzanian guides and porters and gave sage advice, especially the words, "*pole, pole*," which means slowly in Swahili. They emphasized that you had to climb *pole, pole*, acclimating slowly to exertion at elevation, or you risked severe altitude sickness and possibly something worse. The advice proved to be very prophetic a few days later.

I gave the organizer a letter of introduction from my travel agent, which explained why I was climbing and that I needed to summit. He said he would assign me, Diane, and Jerry to William, his most senior and experienced leader. I thanked him, and told him that I simply had to succeed. For me, stand on the summit, or nothing.

The next morning, we all bused a couple of miles up the road to park headquarters, where we received our climbing permits. From there, a trail by foot the entire way, almost 70 miles. After a few hours along the trail, I began to silently worry. I felt tired, despite all the training. I wasn't even at the first climbing hut, Mandara, our destination for the night, and I was tired, with rubbery legs. I didn't share my concern with anyone, but I was worried.

The second day went much better. We hiked upward through a dense cloud forest, the moss, ferns, and epiphytes all dripping wet. Then beyond into the ultramontane plateau, where weirdly shaped lobelia, senecios trees, and other strange vegetation loomed up through the mist like cartoon creatures. I felt so energized that I was probably hiking too quickly. A porter passed me on the trail, smiled, and said, "*Pole, pole.*" "*Asante*," I said, using the Swahili I learned before the trip to say thank you. Maybe the legs would be all right, after all.

On the third day, we finally got a first look at Kilimanjaro, towering above us as we entered the treeless saddle between Kili, as the guides say, and Mt. Mawenzi. On and on we labored upward through the volcanic scree, and the mountain never seemed to get closer. Eventually, I could see the little speck at the base of the mountain that would be our stop, the Kibo Hut, at just under 16,000 feet.

As we ascended toward the hut, other climbers near me began to stagger and visibly slow down. A few even collapsed on the trail. I conversed one moment with a young, vigorous Welshman as we hiked, and the next, he began to slur his words, completely disoriented. Altitude sickness attacked some of the fittest people on the trek, ones who had charged up the trail ahead of the rest of us. *Pole, Pole.*

The porters gave us a meal of some kind of African stew, and we all found our bunks, trying to sleep off the exhaustion. Sleep was next to impossible though, listening in the darkened hut to climbers getting ill from altitude sickness. I had brought with me an old-fashioned Sony Walkman with a cassette tape of music that I hoped would inspire me and take my mind off the fear that I might be the next one sick. The themes from the movies *Superman* and *Raiders of the Lost Ark* played through my headphones over and over.

I said a silent prayer, not really knowing whether I believed in anything or not, but so afraid of failure after all the work to reach that moment. I asked for help, for sustenance that would keep me from letting down everyone back home. All too soon, William tapped me on the shoulder to whisper that it was time to start, in the dark, at one o'clock.

Jerry and I set out with William in the bitter cold. We wanted to be first up and leading. We made the decision the night before that Diane would climb alone with her own guide, at a much slower and safer pace.

I plodded along behind William, remembering an essential element of my training regimen. Before leaving home, I read the recent book, *Seven Summits*, by Dick Bass, the first man to summit the highest peaks on all seven continents. His advice when you were too tired to take another step was to mentally focus by reciting poetry, over and over. A syllable for each step.

I used the last stanza of Alfred Lord Tennyson's *Ulysses*. Forget how utterly exhausted I was, how hungry, how sore—just focus on step after step. "The-lights-be-gin-to-twink-le-from-the-rocks, the-long-day-wanes, the-slow-moon-climbs." A poem about warriors pushing themselves to the limit one more time. On and on, higher and higher, until the last line. "To-strive, to-seek, to-find, and-not-to-yield." Then I repeated it, hour after hour, syllable after syllable, in an almost Zen-like trance to take my mind off the cold and exhaustion.

In the stillness of the night, the only sounds were the crunching of our boots on the volcanic path. But we could hear climbers starting out far below us. Many of them staggered out of the hut, tried to climb, and simply gave up, too sick to make it.

Kilimanjaro is a massive, extinct volcano. To reach the summit, you first crest at Gilman's Point, on the rim of the crater. The actual summit is a mile beyond, and 700 feet higher. I couldn't see Gilman's in the dark, and even with my motivational recitation driving me upward, I began to lose energy. *Had I come so far to stumble now?*

Maybe it was the thin air and low oxygen, the lack of food, or just overall tiredness, but suddenly, an angelic vision materialized. I had not thought of her in months, and there she was, the little girl in the pink dress, the one with her crutches in front of Children's, right there before me. I muttered aloud, "Come on, honey, give me a push. I'm doing this for you."

Whatever happened next, I felt invigorated, as if a hand was gently pushing me from behind. I renewed the drive to Gilman's. Jerry followed me to the point, and we took a brief break to watch the magnificent sunrise over Mawenzi and the Indian Ocean beyond. After a little food and water, I stood up and prepared to summit.

Jerry said, "Wayne, I'm done. I'll wait for you here." I told him I understood. "It's OK, but there's no other option for me. I have to make the top," I said, and started out. A few steps later, Jerry caught up and said he thought he could make it, too.

It was bitterly cold on the exposed ridge to the summit. As we got closer, I could see the sign indicating the highest point in Africa and teared up, thinking of why I was there. The tears never flowed; far too cold for that. I had no idea why, but the next thought that came to me was of all those who had tormented me when I was younger. Would those who had hurled the insults and mocked the walk have made it this high? "Where are you now, you bastards?" I asked out loud to no one but me.

That day, Tanzania had only been independent for 26 years, after an eternity of colonial subjugation. On their first Independence Day in 1961, runners carried a flaming torch from the capital of Dar es Salaam all the way to the mountain. A young Tanzanian army officer cradled the torch to the top of the mountain and lit a massive bonfire. Lights in every town and village for a hundred miles around had been turned off so that everyone could see the light on the mountain top. The first president of the country, Julius Nyere, issued this proclamation at the same time: "We the people of Tanzania would like to light a candle and put it on top of Mt. Kilimanjaro, which would shine beyond our borders, giving hope where there was despair, love where there was hate, and dignity where before there was only humiliation." I knew the story, and found the brass plaque on the summit containing the presidential proclamation.

Jerry and I unfurled the little banner Children's had made for me, and Jerry took pictures of me holding it. I buried the list of all who had contributed to the climb and the picture of the little boy with spina bifida in the volcanic rocks, and then started down. A long 7,000 feet and many miles below, the Horombo Hut stood, where we would spend the night.

We finally arrived at the hut, enveloped by a foggy mist and fading light, completely exhausted and completely exhilarated. We had little airline bottles of scotch with us for just that moment of celebration. I also had brought along a good cigar, carried for victory, lit it, and put on my headphones with the inspirational music. I looked out at Africa somewhere below the clouds, in disbelief at the accomplishment.

The words of the plaque on top came back to me as I puffed on my victory cigar. I couldn't help but apply them to what I was trying to do for Children's. I allowed myself the simple indulgence of believing that if I brought hope where there had been despair to just one sick child, everything had been worth it.

CHAPTER 29

COME ON DOWN

The next morning was our last day, a simple long march downhill to the park headquarters. I put on the T-shirt Children's had given me with the hospital's name on it and a pair of shorts. I had not failed Children's, so I could finally let the rest of the climbers know why I was on the trek. I almost never wore shorts in public; too embarassed by the constant stares at my leg. I put them on and said to myself, I know what I accomplished, I don't care anymore about the stares, or what a stranger thinks.

Hours later, Jerry and I were trudging along, comparing how painful our knees were. One of mine was about to explode. Charging up the trail toward us marched a group just starting out. We stopped to chat with a couple of fellows in the lead, both Australians. They asked if we had summited. We replied that we had. I advised them to pace themselves and noticed one look down at my leg. I knew what he was thinking. If this guy can make it, I will, easily. "We're Aussies, mate, we'll summit. No worries," he said. "Well, *pole, pole*, mate," I said, and down we went.

That night at the Kibo Hotel, many of us in the group had a last celebration dinner together. Only about a quarter of those who started the trek actually summited, and a number of them sitting there had not made it to the top. I wanted to tell them how important it was that we had all tried. I stood up to make a toast, first looking over at the wall displaying banners from some of the most famous climbing clubs in the world. There in the middle hung the banner of Children's that I had carried to the top.

Almost overcome with emotion, I told them why I had climbed. I mentioned the poem I had recited over and over during the climb, and why I did. I told them we had sought out and found something about ourselves by trying, whether we made it all the way to the top or not. We strove together, and we had not yielded. Then we all raised glasses and I offered this toast to them, the same poem:

> The lights begin to twinkle from the rocks;
> The long day wanes; the slow moon climbs; the deep
> Moans round with many voices. Come, my friends,
> 'Tis not too late to seek a newer world.
> Push off, and sitting well in order smite
> The sounding furrows; for my purpose holds
> To sail beyond the sunset, and the baths
> Of all the western stars, until I die.
> It may be that the gulfs will wash us down;
> It may be we shall touch the Happy Isles,
> And see the great Achilles, whom we knew.
> Though much is taken, much abides; and though
> We are not now that strength which in old days
> Moved earth and heaven, that which we are, we are —
> One equal temper of heroic hearts,
> Made weak by time and fate, but strong in will
> To strive, to seek, to find, and not to yield.

CHAPTER 30

POLITICAL AND OTHER ADVENTURES

Within a week of our return in the fall of 1987, voters elected to the city council the candidate whom I had worked for as a volunteer. Ron Roberts was an architect and planner making his first try for elective office. We formed a close bond during the long days and nights of campaigning, and when he won, he asked me to go to work for him as his chief policy advisor. I eagerly accepted, ready to plunge into every big policy issue the city faced. And there were a lot of them. Controlling rampant development, overhauling the crumbling metropolitan sewage system, trying to relocate the airport, downtown development, relations with the U.S. Navy—those and many other important issues all landed on my desk.

Ron operated at a frenetic pace, accepting ownership of every challenging topic. A local reporter once wrote that he was "a man that never met an issue he didn't like." I followed along gladly, happy to work on big issues. An exhilarating, but exhausting time. I frequently put in 16-hour days, but that's what I wanted to do. In the meantime, I received a graduate-level education in every issue affecting cities that one could imagine. And a PhD in the dark arts of what it takes to win, and sometimes lose, politically.

Ron ultimately ended up with a long political career, serving 31 years as either a city councilmember or member of the San Diego County Board of Supervisors. After a couple of very intense years with him, I received an offer for another job, executive director of San Diegans, Inc., a non-profit business organization promoting downtown San Diego. I leapt at the chance to have a more prominent role for myself in shaping local policy. Together with a dynamic board of business leaders, we re-invigorated what had become a moribund organization. Being the face of the entity made for an exciting time, as I met with the press, spoke at public hearings, and lobbied elected officials. My already healthy ego probably didn't need the boost that it got.

During those years, I also became a kind of ambassador for Children's. I served as honorary chair of various local fundraising events for them, spoke at numerous public events, and attended strategic meetings with other volunteers and staff. Every time I went to the hospital for an event, my heart broke seeing the little patients, but soared when I thought that maybe they would one day climb their own mountain. I remained gratified and honored that Children's considered me one of the family.

I continued to think of ascending other mountains. Almost on a whim, a friend and I in 1989 decided to climb Mt. Rainier, outside of Seattle. It's a difficult and dangerous mountain, one that has witnessed many climber deaths, either due to accidents or the weather.

We signed up with a famous Northwest guide service and arrived at their headquarters ready to conquer. Rainier required technical gear, like crampons and ice axes. The guides recommended what were called double plastic boots to effectively hold the crampons. Stiff like ski boots and quite expensive, we decided to simply rent them from the service, as did most of the other climbers. In my case, it proved to be a fateful decision.

I had a good boot fit, and didn't notice anything through the next day's training session. We hiked and climbed much of the day, practicing techniques we would need on the mountain. Being roped together, ice axe arrests if a fellow climber fell, pressure breathing, putting the crampons on and off, and banging on the boots with the ice axe to free the crampons of snow and ice. The boots felt fine. On the way back down to the base, one guide pulled me aside and said he noticed my limp. He asked if I could really make the ascent. I told him about my other climbs and assured him that I was fine. I thought I was.

We set out together the next day to climb up to Camp Muir, at 10,000 feet, where we would spend the night. Like most mountain climbs, there really wasn't much of a night to spend. Climbing starts in the darkness in order to ascend when the snow and ice are firm and the sun hasn't melted it, creating hazardous conditions such as ice breaking into an avalanche. About all we did was go over our gear, have a rudimentary meal, and try to sleep a little before beginning shortly after midnight.

The call came all too soon to assemble for the start. I didn't notice anything in particular getting back into my boots, just a little tingling in each foot. The tingling signaled the problem, but I wasn't astute enough to listen. I checked my step-in harness, carabiners, ice axe, the rest of the gear, and felt ready to go.

The night was dark, cloudy, cold, and very quiet. Roped up together behind the guide, we trudged upward, exhaling with each step to force more air into our lungs, banging on the hard plastic boots to shake off the ice forming. The tingling in my feet became little daggers of pain. I knew then I might be in trouble, but thought I could just grit my way through it.

We finally reached our first stopping point, Disappointment Cleaver. A wide ledge on the side of the mountain where climbers can sit down and rest before the final ascent to the top, a couple of thousand feet above. An apt name, too, because it's where so many climbs aborted due to weather, or climbers who just weren't able to finish.

The first rays of morning light turned the glaciated slopes below us a soft pink. A beautiful moment, except for my problem. I sat on the icy ledge, disappointed all right, eating an energy bar, sipping water, and trying to ignore the pain. I should have put moleskin patches on my feet at every contact point with the boots the night before. When the guide came by after a few minutes to check on each of us, I had to be honest. "Let's take a look," he said. "All right, but I'm afraid I won't be able to get the boots back on." I reluctantly took them off. Little pools of blood were already forming through my socks, everywhere the boots rubbed. We both agreed that I couldn't go on.

A group of us who weren't going to summit descended with one guide, and the others pressed on. By the time we arrived back at Muir Camp, my feet were screaming. Each step a new shot of pain. We waited for those that summited to arrive, and then started down to the base. They assigned a young guide to stay with me, knowing my descent would be painfully slow. I was bitterly frustrated to think that I didn't summit, not because of my leg, but simply because I hadn't prepared my feet properly.

I finally made base camp and changed out of the tortuous boots. Kaye was waiting at the bottom for me and my climbing friend. Over a few beers in the lodge, I contemplated the experience. Sometimes in life we're dealt a setback or failure through no fault of our own. Sometimes, through our own fault for failing to prepare. And sometimes, despite all the attempts at grit and perseverance, we just have to accept the inevitable and end the battle.

CHAPTER 31

JUNGLE ADVENTURE AND MORE

Not long after the Mt. Rainier climb, I felt the need for more adventure. Despite changing jobs and all of the challenges the new position presented, the old urge to travel, to experience something new, lurked. I wanted to do something different. The deep jungles of the Amazon region had fascinated me since childhood. Jungle it would be.

After doing some research, I decided on a trip to the Andean country of Ecuador, the eastern half of which is all jungle, and the headwaters of the Amazon River. Although a small country as South American countries go, Ecuador offered a microcosm of the entire continent. A beautiful coastline and offshore islands, old colonial cities and towns dripping with history and culture, ethnic villages, spectacular volcanic mountains in the Andean high- lands, and, of course, jungle.

Kaye didn't want to accompany me, as the thought of the oppressive jungle heat and humidity repelled her. Despite growing up in South Texas, she'd never done well in those conditions. My diving trips never interested her, either, as those were also in tropical environments.

I arrived in the capitol city of Quito to begin the trip. Once acclimated to the 9,350-foot elevation, the old colonial part of the city showed a glimpse back in time to another era. I wandered through crumbling buildings, some hundreds of years old, with beautiful ornate facades. That historic district later became a UNESCO World Heritage site. I stood at one building in particular, beneath the balcony where Simón Bolívar's mistress would appear to wave at the Liberator and his troops mustered below on horseback, on their way to battle the Spanish overlords.

The Andean highlands swirled with a blend of sights and sounds. Old working haciendas and little villages where local Indians still spoke Quechua, not Spanish, and ate roasted guinea pigs, or *cui*. Local boys in traditional woven ponchos herded their sheep by the side of the road, while alpacas marched alongside to guard the flock. A native group playing ethnic pan flute music at every stop.

A snow-capped Andean volcanic peak appeared in whatever direction I looked. I traveled up to the base of one of them, Cotopaxi. At nearly 20,000 feet, the tallest still – active volcano in the world. The guide and I stood alone at the base, taking in the rarified air and silence. Then, he pointed skyward. HIgh above, a giant Andean condor circled us, a rare sight even for locals. "You're a lucky boy to see this," he said.

Otavalo, in the north of the country, had perhaps the greatest Indian market in the world. Filled with natives, all authentically dressed, buying and selling local produce and handmade goods and generally ignoring the tourists. Tourists were there, of course, but the market was genuinely local.

The most exciting event in the high country happened just by riding the ancient Ecuadorian Express train. Railroad *aficionados* from all over the world came to witness the old steam locomotive hauling a few passenger cars and a caboose through some of the most difficult railway terrain anywhere. They called one particular traverse the Devil's Nose, still considered a railroad engineering marvel to this day. The train literally pulled into a special side track, then backed its way slowly downhill to navigate one of the incredibly steep curves through the mountains.

I passed through Cuenca, a beautiful colonial town where all authentic Panama hats are made, and the grubby port city of Guayaquil before flying back to Quito to start my Amazon exploration. A group of about fifteen of us gathered at the airport for that week-long trip. We boarded a small prop plane to fly over the Andes, almost eye-level with the towering peaks, down to the tiny village of Coca. There, staff from the jungle lodge met us, helping everyone to load into long wooden boats with a roaring outboard motor. The ride up the Rio Napo River, one of the major tributaries to the Amazon River, lasted for hours and many miles.

Eventually, we arrived at a little wooden dock and disembarked for a short hike through the jungle. We came to a large lake, with La Selva on the opposite shore. La Selva, Spanish for the jungle, was an early eco-lodge, entirely self sufficient. It consisted of one large, central building and a collection of little wooden huts with palm-frond roofs and woven-mat walls, everything on stilts and wooden walkways above the swampy edge of the lake.

Every day for a week, we took hikes through the muddy jungle to visit a different wildlife outlook. One not too far from the lodge just enthralled me. A massive kapok tree had a small observation deck built on the top, and a rickety set of wooden steps attached to the trunk to get up there. The tree elevated above the forest canopy, so the deck afforded an unimpeded view. In every direction, an ultra-green jungle extended as far as the eye could see, with no evidence of humans anywhere. One deep breath of the incredibly humid and fetid jungle air felt as if I were at the dawn of civilization.

I went back one afternoon by myself without telling anyone from the lodge, leaving the guides worried and irritated. Not the best idea to be hiking alone in the jungle through the late afternoon shadows, possibly losing the trail, but I had to experience the deck again—alone. I sat there enchanted, loving the interaction with nature. In the distance, a roaring sound. The roars grew nearer, and to a crescendo as a large troop of howler monkeys passed through the treetops right next to me. Iridescent tropical birds of every possible color and shape flew by, or landed on the deck to observe me. That location in the Amazon had recorded more than 500 different species of birds, as high as any observation site in the world.

The highlight of the week came on the day we took small wooden boats up through smaller tributary rivers and even smaller streams. One guide in the front whacked furiously with a machete at the dense growth to allow us through. We reached a little beach clearing where we had lunch, and those of us who wanted to fish got into small wooden dugouts with a native guide.

We targeted the piranha that were everywhere. The guide, from an indigenous tribe in an area where headhunting was once known to exist, spoke only a few words of Spanish. He and I poled through the dense underbrush while we communicated mainly with hand signals. When we stopped, he baited a single hook with a chunk of raw meat and passed me the hand-line. Soon, I had a bite, and hauled up a very angry piranha. He waved at me not to touch it, and reached over to remove the hook. The furious fish lunged at his hand, showing a mouthful of little dagger teeth.

I caught several more, and the guide strung them together on a thin branch from an overhead vine. The piranha continued to try to bite their way through the stick. Back at the lodge that night, the staff served them to me for dinner. Delicious, with a trout-like flavor. I've caught many fish in my life, but nothing more memorable than those little devils.

After dinner, we retired early to our huts, because the lodge had no electricity for lights. A temporary generator provided some power, but at night, we moved around by kerosene torches or flashlights. I said goodnight to the young English couple in the next hut and prepared for bed. A blood-curdling scream pierced the still night. I grabbed my flashlight and scrambled to their hut in time to see a tarantula the size of my fist crawling across the woman's bed. Welcome to the jungle.

CHAPTER 32

BILL AND WAYNE'S
EXCELLENT ADVENTURE

The next year, 1993, my old college roommate, Bill, and I decided to get back into serious scuba diving. We picked the Bay Islands, offshore from Honduras, and booked a dive resort right on the beach on the island of Roatán.

I flew down first, to the capital, Tegucigalpa. After a couple of days of sightseeing and hiking in a nearby rain forest, I hired a driver to take me to the center of the country. We finished the day-long trip at a mountain lake, Lago de Yojoa, where I hoped to catch a legendary peacock bass.

My limited itinerary allowed only one night at the tiny lakeside resort. At first light, a guide took me out in a little boat across the lake, to the far shore lined with a dense tropical forest. We trolled slowly along it, casting at lily pads for the bass. In the trees, a large, beautiful toucan flew from perch to perch, occasionally squawking, keeping exactly even with us as we moved. A beautiful fishing experience, and although I only hooked one bass, who quickly spit the hook, an unforgettable morning.

Bill and I linked up in San Pedro Sula and flew out the next morning to the island for a week of diving. The clear Caribbean waters of Roatán were spectacular, containing an astonishing array of coral, sponges, and fish. Every day, we dove all morning and spent the afternoon loafing in hammocks with a tropical cocktail and a book. A very relaxing way to do a diving trip—until it wasn't.

The big moment of the week came one night. The dive resort had an organized night diving program, taking advantage of a shallow shelf offshore before the reef's edge and the deep drop-off, thousands of feet below. Divers could grab gear, wade out from shore in the dark, and follow a permanent cable to deeper water. The first divers of the night carried a flashing underwater light, affixing it to the end of the cable. From there out to deeper water, it was underwater flashlights only. There were two sunken wrecks, one an old airplane and the other a small tramp freighter, placed to create an artificial reef for sea life.

On the way to the freighter, I turned my flashlight off to experience the darkness. Up, down, sideways—total blackness, except for Bill's light. A very different diving experience, and more than a little intimidating.

We swam back and forth through the eerie, empty rooms of the freighter, as if floating through a graveyard. Above the deck, I motioned to Bill that we should move on to see other things. As I swam away, my flashlight failed. I turned to look for Bill, and nothing. Nothing but blackness.

The number one rule in diving is the buddy system. You stay within eyesight proximity of your dive buddy at all times. Especially at night. I hovered in the same position, panicked at what to do. Still, nothing but darkness.

It seemed like an eternity, but just as I was contemplating surfacing in order to locate the shore, Bill's light flashed across my face. I later found out he knew the direction I had motioned for us to swim, but simply dropped over the other side of the ship to head that way. The hulk blocked his light completely as he lingered, looking at sponge formations on the hull. The drinks back on shore never tasted so good.

Any lingering, slight disappointment I had about Bill not diving next to me that night disappeared the following day. Our dive boat dropped the group off at the edge of the reef, and told us to drift with the current back to where the boat would wait. We floated along the edge, occupied with the coral formations and massive barrel sponges, as large as a human. Very comfortable diving, until out of the corner of my eye, something big swam by.

We were already down about 90 to 100 feet, but the large green sea turtle that just went by me was headed deeper. He swam beautifully, looked back at me, and seemed to wave a flipper to follow along. Before I knew it, I was descending rapidly after him. Far deeper than I should have been.

One of the greatest dangers in diving is nitrogen narcosis, when the nitrogen amount you've been breathing underwater clouds your perception at depths of around 100 feet. At that depth, the partial pressure of nitrogen increases, and can become narcotic. It's also known as "rapture of the deep," for that reason. You feel pleasantly giddy, with your thought process muddled.

Clearly affected, I thought nothing of just swimming after the turtle. Down we went, deeper and deeper, the turtle just evading my reach, until I felt something pulling back on my fin. I turned, and it was Bill, urgently signaling me to stop and for us to ascend. Back on shore, the drinks really, really tasted good that time. I had never experienced nitrogen narcosis before, and never have since. Despite the drinks, I had a sobering moment. Bill quite probably had saved my life.

CHAPTER 33

BACK TO THE FUTURE

I left San Diegans, Inc. in 1993 after we merged it with another organization, creating a more powerful advocacy group, the Downtown San Diego Partnership. The deputy mayor, Tom Behr, asked me to be his chief of staff as he finished his last year in office, and back to city hall I went. Big policy issues still loomed, and I had fun returning to the action.

My involvement in local issues led to increased volunteer activity in the community, too. My neighborhood elected me twice to the local community planning board. Additionally, the mayor, city council, and city manager asked me to serve on various task forces. I put in hundreds, if not thousands, of volunteer hours over the years trying to contribute to a better community, a way of giving back that I found very gratifying.

When the deputy mayor's term expired, I re-activated my bar license and went back to work in the private sector as an attorney. The family business needed help, and other clients materialized over time. I managed to make a living on my own while continuing to be involved in volunteer work for my city.

Several years passed without any new adventurous travel, but Kaye and I did make a wondrous trip to England to spend an old-fashioned Christmas. We drove on Christmas Eve to Oxford, wandering among the old university buildings and the open-air public market, where locals were buying their provisions for the holiday feast. By late afternoon, we arrived in the little village of Woodstock, near Blenheim Palace, the birthplace of Winston Churchill.

The whole setting appeared like a scene on a Christmas card. We stayed in a beautiful coaching inn from the sixteenth century, decorated everywhere with vines of holly and mistletoe. The kind of place where the manager rushed out to help with our luggage the moment we pulled up, and thrust a warming glass of port into our hands when we stepped inside.

That night, we walked through a light snowfall to the little village church for midnight service, drawn by the pealing of hand-rung bells. We sang traditional carols with other worshipers, and the minister's homily about faith and love in the Christmas season moved me. I began to feel the stirrings of faith again after so long. The hot-mulled wine and mince pie waiting for us at the inn may have fueled some of those feelings, too.

Before we left the area, I had to visit the tiny village of Bladon. Behind the little village church, I walked alone through the cemetery in a cold, drizzly rain until I found them. The family burial plots of the Churchills. I teared up standing in front of Winston Churchill's grave, humbled to be there in front of one of the greats of history, buried in such a modest place.

Back home again, I continued my involvement with local politics. My old political boss, Ron Roberts, by then a county supervisor, was running for mayor of San Diego. I served on his steering committee and tried to contribute to the campaign in any way I could. When he finished first in the primary by a wide margin, it looked like I might be returning to a major policy role with the mayor's office if he won in the fall. Somehow, despite being a prohibitive early favorite in the general election, he didn't win. The whole campaign went from ecstatic to anguished in just a matter of months. That's the adventure of politics. Nothing is ever certain.

I decided to get as far away as possible and settled on Turkey. An American friend lived there, married to a Turkish fellow. I stayed with them in Istanbul a few days, roaming all over the city. Then I took off to see the country by myself, taking local buses and stopping wherever I felt like it. The beauty of the countryside, friendly people, and blend of history and culture all were captivating. History infused everything, with ancient ruins resting alongside Byzantine buildings, next to Ottoman-era sites.

I booked two separate tours on one special day. In the morning, a group of us visited crumbled ancient Troy, where some parts of the old city walls still stand, 5,000 years old. In the afternoon, another tour took a group across the narrow Dardanelles strait to the Gallipoli battlefield from World War I, an epic turning point in the war. That day alone spanned 5,000 years, and the experience of visiting two of the most significant battle sites of all time.

I stopped in Ephesus a couple of days later to view the incredible Greek and Roman ruins. Walking down the marbled cobblestone main street toward the library of Celsus was literally walking in the footsteps of the apostle Paul. Shopkeepers lined that street when he visited, selling amulets and other religious symbols of pagan Roman gods. They physically attacked him as a Christian, and as such, bad for business.

Then I toured the ruins of the Temple of Artemis, one of the seven wonders of the ancient world. Only one original marble pillar remained upright from the many that once supported a massive structure. In ancient times, the temple was already hundreds of years old when an arsonist burned it down. Alexander the Great himself ordered it rebuilt as his army marched by on their way to invading Persia.

On the hill behind the ruined temple stood the Basilica of St. John, built by the Byzantines, and worshipped as the burial place of the apostle John. When Turkey converted to Islam centuries later, the site became a mosque, but a very important one architecturally. They kept the Byzantine style, a rarity in the Muslim world.

From the cross, Jesus instructed the apostle to take care of his mother, Mary. John brought her to this place, and she is believed by the faithful to be buried just a few miles away in the hills. To stand there and contemplate the conflict, the faith, and the history that occurred in just that one spot overwhelmed and humbled at the same time.

Buses carried me farther south, down to the Turquoise Coast. Everywhere, history permeated, a real treat for a college history major and life-long history buff like me. I visited the mausoleum of Halicarnassus in Bodrum, another one of the seven wonders of the ancient world. Later, the ghost city of Patara, abandoned for centuries and almost covered by sand dunes. Patara was the home of the real Santa Claus. St. Nicholas actually lived there as the local bishop in the 4th century A.D., before his martyrdom.

I stopped long enough in Peralta to book a scuba diving trip. The waters were in fact turquoise, but a disappointment. Not much to see, although the clear, warm water seemed almost therapeutic. In the mountains above the town were Lycian ruins, where I walked among stone sarcophagi thousands of years old. The Lycians left their dead on top of the stone structures to be devoured by birds. They died out as a kingdom millennia ago; perhaps their strange customs contributed to that.

Back in Istanbul, I had a last-night drink with my friends at the Perra Palace, the historic hotel where Agatha Christie wrote *Murder on the Orient Express*. We walked to the nearby Galata Tower, built in the 14th century by the Genoans as a fortress to protect their Crusader plunder, stolen both from Byzantium and the Holy Land. From the observation deck, I looked out at the bustling Bosporus, the Sea of Marmara beyond, and all of minareted Istanbul. Below us, the setting sun burnished the Golden Horn truly golden. It had been a magical trip.

The long flight home afforded me many hours to ponder what came next. Was there any future for me in politics? If not, what could I do with my life to make a difference, to feel like I was contributing something? Was I traveling merely to check countries off a list, or to truly experience them and by doing so, experience myself? I didn't realize it at the time, but I was searching for meaning, and looking for it in the wrong places.

CHAPTER 34

LIFE AND DEATH INTERVENE

As the end of the year 2000 approached, I needed to make some decisions. The city council seat in the district where I lived and had worked in at city hall would be coming open due to term limits. The state scheduled the primary for a full 14 months away, but political background noise told me that others were already gearing up for the race. I had done everything in city government except being the actual councilmember, and everything possible out in the community as a volunteer. I thought no other potential candidate had a better history or résumé, so if I was ever going to round out my career with an elected office, it certainly seemed like the time.

I began talking with community leaders and elected officials early in the new year, just trying to test the waters. Receiving encouraging feedback, I made a preliminary commitment to myself to run. Clearly, though, it would be a very competitive race, as I heard other candidates were already lining up supporters.

One morning, I finished a breakfast meeting with a community leader, then drove to the family business. I still did occasional outside legal work for it, and showed up there frequently. When I walked into Dad's office, brother Glenn sat there, too. The mood wasn't just somber, it was funereal.

"Mike's been in a bad accident," Glenn said. Our younger brother Mike also worked for the company and was on a business trip to Central California that day. I asked how he knew, and he told me that a good Samaritan at the accident site found company literature in Mike's truck and called the listed phone number.

Mike had been on his way to repair one of the company's products, a small electrical generation system, and left home before dawn to beat the Los

Angeles area traffic. His 19-year old son, Ray, who often accompanied him to help with repairs, was sleeping in a camper shell in the back of the truck, with their dog alongside him.

When the good Samaritan called, he told Dad that Mike had been life-flighted by helicopter to an area hospital. Dad scrambled to leave as I got there, planning to drive straight to the hospital, about 90 miles away. We gave him a borrowed cell phone and asked him to call us as soon as he got there, if he could get the phone to work.

Glenn and I looked at each other and knew there was nothing we could do but wait. We also knew that Mom had planned to come by the shop that morning, so we would have to tell her. When she arrived, we hugged her and told her the bad news. After her initial shock, she immediately showed her usual positivity and said, "OK, we'll get him fixed up."

While she was out of the room, Glenn took a call from the hospital. I stood next to him to listen. "Yes, I understand. Thank you for calling," he said. Despite the frantic efforts to save him, Mike died shortly after arriving. We had no way to tell Dad, but the hospital assured us they would have grief counselors there to meet him.

The day stretched longer as we sat there waiting for more news. Mom softly crying. The next call we received came from the California Highway Patrol. The officer explained what had happened. While Mike drove down the freeway, the turnbuckles that held the camper shell to the bed of his pickup failed, and the entire shell, with Ray and their dog inside, flew off and into another freeway lane. Mike pulled into the median and desperately ran into the freeway to stop traffic. He was going to try to push the shell to safety. Ray, trapped inside by the crushed door, screamed for help.

All of the traffic screeched to a halt, and several drivers jumped out to help. All except one woman, apparently oblivious after working an all-night shift. She didn't try to slow down until it was too late. Mike could see her coming, according to one witness, because his last words were, "Oh, shit!" Her car drove the shell into Mike's head, and he died from blunt-force trauma to the brain.

When we finally got a call from Dad, he had kissed Mike goodbye and gone to another hospital to find Ray. Miraculously, Ray survived with just severe bruises. They went together to a veterinary hospital to pick up the dog, who also had survived and drove home. We all gathered at Mom and Dad's place that night to embrace one another, trying to make sense of what had happened. We tried to comfort the dog, too, but she couldn't move her hind legs. They took her in the morning to a veterinarian, who put her down after discovering that she broke her back in the crash and was paralyzed. Her name, prophetically—Trouble.

Eventually, I made it home that night, too drained to think or do anything. Although I saw Mike frequently at the factory, he and I had not been close for years. I sat down and his smiling face flashed in front of me, turning around in the front of the canoe to encourage me as we paddled down the Colorado, so many years before. I put my head down and wept.

I finally went to bed and prayed with a sincerity that had been missing for a very long time. I didn't know if anyone was listening, but I prayed for his mortal soul. I asked for comfort for Mom and Dad, and tried to sleep. Sometime during a troubled night, I awoke with a start. There, at the door to the bedroom, was Mike, staring at me with angry, flaming green eyes. When I tried to speak to him, he disappeared, forever.

CHAPTER 35

MORE ADVENTURES IN POLITICS

In the weeks after Mike's death, I had serious reservations about continuing to run for office. I knew my heartbroken parents would need help sorting out Mike's affairs. I also knew my heart and head weren't really into it, a bad sign for any campaign.

My meetings with community leaders, elected officials, and campaign professionals continued, and still went well. Many of them encouraged me to commit, citing the need to make a firm start. Even though the primary was a full year away, in March 2002, others were already aggressively campaigning.

One meeting in particular excited me. I met with a well-known local political consultant. He told me that I would be the "class of the field," and that he wouldn't want to work for anyone else. I thanked him and said I would continue to line up supporters and be back in touch. I left with a very positive feeling that a campaign could be successful, knowing that having him on my team would boost my stature as a candidate.

The field of probable candidates appeared beatable. Surveying them, no one had my combination of actual city hall, business, law, and community experience. Once the voters learned that, I wouldn't have any problem emerging as the frontrunner. Or so I thought.

Soon enough, I would learn just how naive I was. I learned that the gap between being a campaign worker on a successful campaign, as I had done many times, and being the actual candidate, which I had never done, was not just a gap, but the Grand Canyon.

My first problem occurred when the professional political fundraisers I thought were on board backed out. They were friends that I had worked with on other winning campaigns, but they made a decision to transition out of politics. I would have to scour the town for someone as competent.

Then, two of the prominent business leaders I had solicited for an endorsement, which I received, reneged on their endorsements. One was Republican and the other a Democrat, both known for their affiliations. The office was non-partisan, and I wanted to run that kind of campaign, with broad support. At least one fellow had the grace to call and apologize, saying he had received a lot of pressure from party types to back another candidate. That's when I realized that no amount of running on the issues would matter—it would be partisan money and backers that decided the race.

Finally, I learned second-hand that the consultant I met with months earlier had signed up with a rival candidate. Despite having told me that he wouldn't want to work for anyone else, and without ever telling me. Welcome to politics when you're the actual candidate.

As summer approached, I needed to make the final decision to commit to a campaign and publicly declare my candidacy. In spite of the setbacks, I still thought it was winnable. I discussed it endlessly with friends who volunteered to help, ones who also had campaigning experience. We concluded that indeed it was winnable, and I started the formal process. By then, I felt the challenge more than anything else—I wanted to climb a different kind of mountain.

I spent the fall months trying to raise money and support. Few things in life are more dispiriting than begging for contributions to a political campaign. After so many years of helping others campaign, donating to their campaigns or causes, helping with their issues, I assumed it would be easy to line up support. Was I ever wrong.

The real slog began when it was time to begin walking precincts door-to-door. Walking had never been particularly easy for me, and grinding along day after day really wore me out physically. Ironically, though, knocking on strangers' doors turned out to be one of the few highlights of the whole experience.

One Saturday afternoon a young man answered his door, completely naked, holding a small towel around his waist with one hand, and a happy grin on his face. He was clearly "engaged" in something else, so I offered to leave immediately. He insisted on taking my campaign literature and thanked me for running.

Another day, I knocked on a door and an older lady opened it and smiled at me with twinkling blue eyes. She said that she had just a minute before finished filling out her absentee ballot, voting for me. A highlight, but maybe not as much as the one from her neighbor down the street. The young woman who answered the door told me she had been following my campaign, especially seeing all of my yard signs in her neighborhood. She gushed that she had been hoping to meet me. "I wanted to tell you what a wonderful name for a champagne you have!" How could I beat that?

I also had doors slammed in my face, thanks to disinformation other candidates peddled. I had a record of involvement with issues facing the district, one I was proud of and that other candidates couldn't match. It was extremely galling to see that record distorted, leaving me bitter and angry at times. A friend added an exclamation point when he sent in a contribution check with a personal note. "Are you crazy?" it read. "Why would you want to be the only fire hydrant in a town with 500 dogs?"

Although there were ultimately eight candidates in the race, realistically only three of us had an honest chance. As we got closer to the primary, I learned that one of the other leaders had heavy backing from Democrats and local unions. Republicans and business interests heavily backed the other leader. I fought on anyway, but I already knew what the inevitable outcome would be. When those two faced off later in the general election, it was then the most expensive city council race ever.

On primary night, I finished a close, respectable third. Because I did so well in a losing cause, supporters of the two runoff opponents deluged me almost immediately. Each side wanted my endorsement, but all I wanted was to get away. Instead of staying involved, I flew alone to Belize a few weeks later, physically and emotionally exhausted.

CHAPTER 36

RENEWAL

After researching Belize online, I booked a small place on an offshore island, Ambergris Caye, right on the beach. I went scuba diving in spectacular waters every morning, read on the sand in the afternoon, and hit a bar or two every night. Nothing quite like ending a warm tropical night on the beach, rustling palm fronds overhead, a frozen drink and Cuban cigar in hand. During the week I spent on the island, the tension, anger, and frustration of the previous year began to melt away.

My most memorable dive day occurred when we dove the Blue Hole. We left the dock from Ambergris Caye before dawn, and headed several hours and many miles out to sea. Arriving at the Blue Hole, a shimmering array of blue and aquamarine colors greeted us. The hole itself formed eons ago when the rising seas collapsed an ancient cave. Descent in the stunningly clear water, down through stalactites along the wall, was like flying through a cave.

We halted at about 160 feet and hung there, suspended and mesmerized. In the center of the hole, maybe 50 feet away, a huge bull shark swam back and forth, eyeing us with suspicion. We ascended slowly, pausing for safety stops because of the depth. At a last stop, the divemaster banged on his tank, the signal for all of us to look at him. He pointed at me, then pointed above me. I looked up, and a very large barracuda, mouth open and razor teeth exposed, hovered over me. He swam languidly away as I continued to rise. Back on the surface, the divemaster told me the big fish ascended with me almost the entire way.

We had two more dive stops to make before returning to Ambergris. The first, a reef off of Lighthouse Caye, where we chased big tarpon through underwater tunnels and beautiful coral. After lunch on the Caye among blue-footed boobies and hordes of big land crabs, a last stop at Shark Ray Alley. We snorkeled the shallow waters among masses of sting rays, all bumping into us while looking for a treat. I couldn't imagine a more adventurous day of diving.

After days of diving, I flew back to the mainland to see more of the region. The first stop was Tikal, Guatemala. Among the most important and impressive of all the Mayan ruin sites, Tikal didn't disappoint. I hired a driver for the day from the old colonial town of Flores, where I spent the night.

We arrived at dawn, the heat and humidity already oppressive. I didn't care. I scrambled up every ruined, vine-covered temple while my rather overweight local guide waited below. The jungle crept in from all directions, but the few ancient buildings already excavated were breathtaking, in more ways than one. All around, hundreds more structures lay buried beneath the fetid canopy of vegetation, many still unmapped. To realize that this once enormous, vibrant city, was almost completely covered in jungle centuries later made me contemplate how fleeting glory is.

The driver dropped me off at the Belize border that night. I stayed several more days in an eco-lodge in the highlands, exploring, hiking, and swimming in a local river. I booked a highlight trip with a guide to visit a sacred Mayan cave. The cave had been discovered just a few decades before, and only open to the public for just a few years.

He and I were the only ones there. A river flowed out of the cave, so we explored it in a tiny wooden boat, barely big enough for the two of us. We entered total darkness within minutes, our path illuminated only by his headlamp. When he shined it on the cave walls, I could see Mayan pottery sitting on ledges, undisturbed for a millennium. At one point, we both had to lie supine in the boat, my nose barely clearing the cave ceiling. We emerged into a giant cavern, and his light fell on a higher ledge. There, the skeleton of what he told me was a young Mayan girl rested in repose, ceremonially buried a 1,000 years before.

Back home, friends commented on how relaxed I looked. The trip refreshed my mind as it hadn't been in more than a year. I couldn't escape the political experience entirely, though. Soon, the campaigns of both final candidates contacted me again to ask for my endorsement. I decided to keep my powder dry and see how the fall election evolved.

The summer wore on, and I knew I had to get some things off of my chest. *San Diego Magazine* agreed to run my proposed article about the experience as a candidate. The article, entitled *Through a Political Looking Glass Darkly,* ran in October, just before the general election. In it, I described a kind of *Through the Looking Glass* environment that occurs when a candidate passes through the political mirror, a scenario where up is down, truth flexible, and old loyalties shifting. What it felt like to have assisted others with their campaigns or causes and assume they would follow me when it was my turn, only to turn around and see no one following.

As I wrote: "The emotional and physical roller coaster can only be appreciated once you have passed through to the other world. In that other world, you know the intoxication of applause after a campaign speech. The absolute high of opening the mail and finding enough checks to continue the fight. The joy of seeing your name in print and feeling your voice is being heard on issues. You also know the lows of opening the mail and seeing your opponents smear your record. Of total strangers calling you on the telephone and yelling at you. Of calls to potential supporters that are never returned. All of these experiences can come in the same day—often day after day."

I concluded by writing that although I wasn't happy with the saga, I wasn't sorry that I had run. I wrote of the comfort the great lines of Theodore Roosevelt gave me: "The credit belongs to the man who is actually in the arena ... who spends himself in a worthy cause ... and if he fails while daring greatly, knows his place shall never be with those timid and cold souls who know neither victory nor defeat."

The day the magazine hit the newsstands, I received a call from an acquaintance, a prominent banker in town. He told me how much he enjoyed the article, and how sorry he was that I hadn't won. "It should be mandatory reading in every Political Science 101 class," he said.

CHAPTER 37

BACK TO THE FUTURE, PART TWO

I transitioned back into working on my own as a lawyer for various clients by the time the fall election cycle ended. I still wanted to be involved in the community, though. The eventual winner, Michael Zucchet, and I became good friends, and he promised to help if an opening for an appointment occurred. Within a few months, a vacancy did open up on one of the most prestigious boards in the city, the redevelopment agency that managed downtown San Diego. With his help, the mayor and council appointed me to fill the slot, and I dove head-first back into land use issues.

I enjoyed the work and spent long hours as a volunteer trying to improve a redeveloping downtown. The councilmember and I remained in close touch, often discussing policy and land use issues. We created a relationship of mutual trust and respect. At the same time, my legal client list grew. Life was going well.

One day, a colleague called to tell me astonishing news. My friend the councilmember and two of his fellow councilmembers had been raided that morning at their city hall offices by the FBI. All three were indicted on a variety of federal charges, mainly involving allegations of bribery. Surreal didn't begin to describe the moment.

Within about an hour, I received the first of what would be many phone calls from very connected political movers and shakers. The caller asked if I had heard the news, and I assured him that I had. He first apologized for not supporting me when I ran, and urged me to jump into what would be a special election when the councilmember eventually resigned, or was removed. He promised me whatever support I would possibly need.

I thanked him with a laugh, and said no. I told him what a difficult experience running had been for me. I finished by saying "When you run for office, you put your dignity at the voters' grace, and doing that once was enough for me."

More calls came in over the next few weeks, but I always gave the same answer. I couldn't help but reflect on the vicissitudes of life. How could anyone have predicted such an outcome? When I attended events around town, invariably someone I knew would approach and tell me how glad I must be that I didn't win. What actually came more to mind was the realization that things do happen for a reason, but usually, we aren't privileged to know that reason.

The more I thought about circumstances, the more that vague spiritual feelings returned. Even if I couldn't know the reason, there was no question in my mind that things indeed happened to me for a reason, and had my whole life. Not long after, I traveled back to Thailand and Southeast Asia. I didn't know when I left how soon my reflections would be reinforced.

Bangkok grabbed me the moment I arrived. Always an exciting place, it pulsated much more dynamically. Scuba diving gave me one reason for returning, so once in the country, I arranged a flight down to the Thai diving hot spot of Phuket. I found comfortable lodgings and a reputable dive shop, ready to try new waters.

The dive boat took us to Ko Phi Phi, a lush, tropical island famous for spectacular karst limestone formations rising straight up out of the waters nearby, and infamous for hordes of young tourists overrunning it. We dove in the same area the next couple of days, enjoying the clear, warm water and beautiful sea life. After diving, I spent my afternoons back in Phuket, loafing on the wooden chaise lounges on the central beach in town.

Nights were fun, filled with good restaurants and lively bars. By sheer luck, my trip coincided with the one night of the year when Thais celebrated *Loi Krathong*, the festival of giving thanks. *Loi Krathong* always occurred on the full moon of the 12th month of the traditional Thai calendar.

The festival centered around celebrants visiting the nearest waterway at night and purchasing a little boat, one typically handmade of banana leaves and holding a lit candle and incense sticks. They made a wish, or prayer, and pushed the boat out to sea or into a river to float away. Not only were they giving thanks, the little boats also floated away the transgressions and problems of the past year.

I bought my own boat and pushed it out to sea, bearing a heavy weight of wishes and hopes for the future. And, maybe a transgression or two. At the same time, hundreds of paper balloons were released on the beach, the heat from the candle hanging below causing them to rise up to the full moon. The whole effect was incredibly beautiful, even considering the remote danger of the balloons floating back over land and setting something on fire.

A few weeks later, Phuket and that whole part of Thailand experienced real, unfathomable danger. An earthquake-spawned tsunami crashed into the entire region, creating an enormous disaster. I had just returned home when it happened, and watched in horror as the nightmarish clips flickered past on TV. Over and over again, networks showed a scene from Phuket. A massive wave carrying the same chaise lounges I had enjoyed on the beach, roaring through the streets of the city. The same beach where just weeks before I sat in the sand and watched those lanterns floating to the heavens during *Loi Krathong*. Hundreds of thousands died along the rim of the Indian Ocean from the event, and at least ten thousand of those were in the Phuket area.

I scoured the internet for days looking for more coverage. One story that I found left me simply incredulous. A British woman had been working as a diving instructor on Ko Phi Phi. When the tsunami struck, she was leading a group of divers in the same waters where I dove just weeks before. They were offshore, fifty feet down, with no warning when it hit. Every diver in her group died, and most were never found. She was discovered, miraculously alive, at the top of a palm tree where the waves had swept her, many yards inland from the beach. Shocked, I could only remind myself that we never truly know the mystery of life, why some things happen, why some survive, and others don't.

CHAPTER 38

ON THE ROAD, AGAIN

By 2006, I wanted to dive again, and thought of Thailand. This time on the other side of the country in the Gulf of Siam. What were the odds there would be another tsunami? I planned to combine the trip with seeing the Southeast Asian countries I had not yet visited, Cambodia, Laos, and Vietnam.

I arrived in Bangkok, and after a couple of days to acclimate, flew down to the island of Ko Samui. From there, a ferry for the hours-long ride out to Ko Tao island. Fellow divers on my previous trip told me that Ko Tao was the best diving in the country. When we docked, my heart sank. Instead of an island paradise, as it was billed, I saw a grubby little main town, crammed with young backpacker tourists. I made my way to the diving resort I had booked, which proved to be an even grubbier affair. I didn't know it at the time, but Ko Tao was known then and still is to this day as "murder island," for the number of mysterious tourist deaths over the years.

They showed me my accommodations at the "resort," and I almost walked straight back to wait for the next ferry anywhere. The island should have been called Ko Toilet. Their diving operation was even worse, mainly geared to making money teaching young European tourists how to dive. I had traveled so far, and there were so many other divers there that I thought, well, just put up with everything, because once you get in the water, the diving must be terrific. It was—terrifically crowded with other divers and dive boats. I saw almost nothing but divers underwater, and after one day cut the visit short and left for Bangkok. Adding to my disenchantment, I spent nearly an entire day at the little Ko Samui airport waiting for any flight out. Monsoonal rains canceled flight after flight, all day long, until I finally caught one of the last ones back.

Cambodia and its ruined cities were as captivating as advertised. Once in country at Siam Riep, I hired a driver and a guide to take me at dawn out to Angkor Wat and the adjacent ruins, Angkor Thom and Ta Prohm. I scrambled almost alone over the magnificent structures in the early hours, the start of a long, stiflingly hot day of exploring. Despite the heat and humidity, just an awesome feeling to stand there under the massive over-grown trees and vines, seeing them still trying to overwhelm the crumbled buildings. I thought if I stood there long enough, a vine might try to enve-lope me, too.

Passing through the unremarkable Vientiane, capital of Laos, I traveled up to Luang Prabang, in the far north of the country. An ancient, sleepy place that had become a UNESCO World Heritage site, Luang Prabang seemed lost in a previous century. Buddhist temples and monks were everywhere. Fading French colonial architecture and a location alongside the muddy Mekong River completed the scene. Although Laos had only recently been opened to tourism, tourists were already there, but not in hordes. Everyone appeared respectful of the culture, slow pace, and history of the place. After several peaceful days there, I moved on again.

I flew into Hanoi in a driving rainstorm and caught a taxi into the Old Quarter. After circling repeatedly through the rabbit warren of old buildings, the driver finally found the street where according to my guide book, a decent, affordable hotel supposedly existed. We identified the address but never dis-covered a hotel. Across the street, though, one looked promising. It turned out to be a beautifully restored boutique hotel that gave me a great rate, and became my headquarters for the week.

The U.S. never bombed the Old Quarter during the Vietnam War, so the historic old buildings were intact. I wandered for hours through the maze of subdistricts, fascinated by the ancient segregation of uses. One street dedi-cated only to metalworkers banging away on their hand-made goods. Another, just paper goods. Turning down another, butchering and produce, with the remains spilling out onto the cobblestones.

The Vietnamese were friendly, particularly the children. They knew instinctively that I was American, so I expected hostility. Instead, amazing friendliness. Little boys would run up to me, smile, and quickly make a peace sign.

One day, I took a guided tour of the city, the highlight of which was a visit to Ho Chi Minh's mausoleum. I stood in line in a torrential downpour for the opportunity of making a rather quick walk past his pickled body. There he reclined in repose, our great enemy from the war, re-embalmed by the Russians annually and looking exactly like those stark photos of him back then. A surreal moment, like the scene I saw the next day.

Hoa Lo prison sits right in the middle of the city. Known during the Vietnam War to Americans as the Hanoi Hilton, it's where our prisoners of war were incarcerated. The Vietnamese government converted it to a museum dedicated more to displays of torture and abuse of Vietnamese political prisoners under their French colonial rulers than to the Americans who were imprisoned there. Knowing that I planned to visit the prison, before I left home I called a friend who had been a prisoner there for many years. I asked if there was anything he would like me to carry back to the site for him. He thought a moment, then said, "How about a bag of shit? That's what I'd like you to take back to them."

Walking the halls and seeing the prison cells where our men were held, tortured, and abused for years affected me deeply. In one room, pictures of those incarcerated hung. Nearby and behind glass stood the flight suit that John McCain wore when he crash-landed in a lake nearby.

I returned to Bangkok for a couple of days before beginning the trip home. The atmosphere in the city seemed normal, if anything in that frenetic place is ever truly normal. Little did anyone on the streets know what was coming.

I broke up the long flight home by stopping for a few days in Tokyo, enjoying the dynamism of the city. The high point came with a guided city tour that ended at the main Shinto temple. At the entrance, the guide explained that according to custom, locals wrote a prayer or wish for good luck on a slip of paper and inserted it into a structure near the altar. He confessed that many of them were from students praying for a passing grade on university exams.

When the tour reached the altar, clouds of incense floated past hundreds of messages already tucked in. The devout and the merely curious milled about. I added a message, too, but a rather different one.

I thought of my late father-in-law, Percy, a man I never had the honor of meeting. He died of cancer a few years before I met Kaye, but I knew his story.

The outbreak of World War II found him serving in the Army Air Corps in the Philippines. Captured near Corregidor, he survived the hell of the Bataan Death March and the horrendous death rate on ships that carried prisoners to Japan. In Japan, he spent the remaining years of the war as a starving slave laborer. "Percy," I wrote, "this is for you. YOU WON!"

I turned on the TV a few days after I returned home and couldn't believe what I saw back in Thailand. The military had executed a coup. Tanks and soldiers prowled the streets of Bangkok, while citizens and tourists cowered out of sight. The elected president of the country fled into exile, and no one was certain of the outcome. It could have been a very dangerous time to be a tourist, desperate to get out of the country. Once again, for whatever reason, I had avoided disaster.

CHAPTER 39

MISADVENTURE AND SALVATION

I settled back in after the trip, but by the next year, 2007, another litigation nightmare overtook everything. A bitter situation had emerged from the company my family once owned, sold, and then operated for a series of owners. The last owner left the business woefully undercapitalized, and despite heroic efforts by my father and brother to keep it viable, including loaning their own money to keep it afloat, it was in trouble.

Nasty allegations flew back and forth as each side lawyered up. The effort to help put together my family's case against the owner overwhelmed me. Months later, that defendant owner amended his case to sue me, too. There was never an allegation criticizing the legal work I had done as outside counsel, merely sleazy implications of guilt by association with my family, and vague conflict-of-interest charges. In any event, I sank deeper and deeper into the morass that is litigation. Over and over again the great quote from Ambrose Bierce's *The Devil's Dictionary* came to my mind: "Litigation is a process by which one enters as a pig, and emerges as a sausage."

After a grueling year of preparation, the trial finally began. Our lawyers did a fine job with a difficult collection of issues and facts. The trial seemed interminable, but on the last day, after closing arguments were over, I felt positive that we had won.

When the decision from the court came out weeks later, we realized what a catastrophic mistake we had made. The lawyers had advised us to waive a jury trial and proceed with just a judge, believing the business litigation might be too complicated for a jury. That left everything in the hands of only one individual. He interpreted almost every issue and made every ruling against us, despite the trial evidence, the testimony, and even the law. It was devastating, and revealed to me the correctness of H.L. Mencken's definition of a judge: "Merely a law student who gets to grade his own exam paper."

We had no choice but to continue fighting on appeal, but when you're on appeal of an adverse decision, you already have one foot in the legal grave. After another year of struggle, we were too emotionally drained, physically exhausted, and financially depleted to continue. We settled what we could settle, on awful terms, and quit appealing elsewhere.

I knew that two and a half years of my life had been wasted. I also knew that the anger and rage in me against anyone connected with either the decision or the other side was beginning to poison my life. I had never before felt such hatred and bitterness, or had such violent fantasies about physically crushing other people.

Throughout the entire litigation process, Kaye had remained a faithful, steadying influence. I was truly sorry to come home every day from the battle and unburden myself to her, but I had to have someone to talk to about the nightmare. In the end, she simply told me to accept the outcome and the financial losses, and just get on with life. She was right.

I took up kayak fishing during that time as a diversion from my raging mental state. I threw myself into the new hobby, relearning how to fish, how to haul the kayak around in my SUV, and experiencing new gear and techniques. The solo kayak provided solitary moments on the water to reflect. I began to see my fishing trips as meditation, an almost Zen-like experience. Launching the kayak at dawn through the surf of a local beach, peddling alone more than a mile offshore, searching for fish, cleared my mind of many things.

One early spring morning, I drove up to Lake Cuyamaca, high in our local mountains and an hour drive east of home. In the gray, predawn light, I slowed down to let a dozen deer cross in front of me. When I launched the kayak, the only fisherman on the lake, a flock of wild turkeys called to each other along the brushy shore. Across the placid water, the first rays of dawn filtered through the towering pine trees. A serene and beautiful moment. Floating alone on the water, I remembered these lines from my college Shakespeare class, his Sonnet 33:

"Full many a glorious morning have I seen
Flatter the mountain tops with sovereign eye,
Kissing with golden face the meadows green,
Gilding pale streams with heavenly alchemy."

Lost in the moment of reverie, I was startled back to reality when my rod suddenly snapped over. The moment of hope and mystery when a fisherman struggles with the twisting rod, never knowing what's on the other end of the line until it's brought in. I caught a nice, fat trout. I fished a while longer, enjoying the bucolic morning. After catching another one, a loud screech above. Overhead, a bald eagle circled me. I pulled the kayak ashore to head home and paused to dwell on all that surrounded me. How could I not appreciate the moment, the beauty, and the nature around me?

Filled with a sense of peace that I hadn't experienced in a very, very long time, maybe I was beginning to put a miserable situation behind me. On the long drive down the mountain, I thought that perhaps God showed me a way forward that morning. If I had actually carried out any of my crazy fantasies about harming the defendant, he would have won a second time, because I would be in jail. It was time to finally purge those thoughts from my mind.

CHAPTER 40

THE ADVENTURE OF FAITH

As time passed, life resumed a level of normalcy. I found myself more and more reflective about everything around me. I felt indeed "... a part of all that I had met," in Tennyson's phrase. So many stories and adventures, so many incredible people met. In private moments, I considered all that I had achieved and experienced, despite the physical challenges.

Did I have regrets? Did I wish that I had been more normal physically, that I had never had polio? No. I could honestly say that not for one moment in my life had I ever wondered or said aloud, "Why me? Why did the wolf attack me, and not others?" It was, and always has been just another challenge. Move forward and try my best. I never wasted a moment thinking about what might have been, I only thought of what was accomplished.

Instead of feeling sorry for myself, the sight of others far more challenged and still succeeding always uplifted me. Where I had a withered, only partially useful leg, some had no leg at all. The heroes in my life were those with enormous physical challenges who not only met those challenges, but embraced them and flourished.

As my contemplative thoughts increased, it led to an epochal moment. Not a Saul on the road to Damascus, lightning bolt epiphany, but rather a slow awakening. After enduring and experiencing so much, there simply had to be a reason, a purpose, to my life. There was—I just had to find it.

Gradually, the truth came to me. I realized that God had indeed answered my childhood prayer. Over and over again, night after night, the same prayer. Please, God, make my leg like the other one. And, every morning, waking up to disappointment. When that moment of truth came, I finally understood that the leg was actually the same as the other one, at least in my mind, and that's all that mattered. What others saw didn't matter. When I thought of all that I had experienced in life, of course the prayer had been answered.

The faint embers of my faith, that perhaps had always been there, glowed a little brighter. I thought back about my youth, especially the college years, when I was a committed atheist. How had I evolved into a believer after being so intellectually convinced that God didn't exist? Back then, I studied every argument for the existence of God in various philosophy classes and rationalized away all of them.

I remembered clearly the Philosophy of Nietzsche class I took in Germany. Reading him in both German and English, I came across this quote: "Christians would sooner have the void for their purpose than be void of purpose." At the time, I understood exactly what he meant and loved the quote, wallowing in his utter cynicism. I used it often in bull sessions with Christian fellow students, convinced there was only the void, and no purpose.

I slowly progressed over the years from the arrogance of atheism to the gnawing doubt of agnosticism. From there, an occasional lonely conversation through prayer, always wondering if anyone was listening.

When I finally understood that someone was indeed listening, I began to pray nightly. I prayed for family and friends, for those that I knew were suffering physically and for their recovery, that those who needed protection would be safe. In general, for blessings on those that I loved. Those prayers continue to this day, but they never include praying for myself. My prayers were answered, long ago.

There is no organized religion in my life. I don't attend a church, consult a minister, or even read the Bible on a regular basis. While that might sound heretical, I have never felt that for me, those aspects of believing were necessary for my faith. Having had a strict upbringing in a traditional Christian family and experiencing all of those elements in depth, I don't believe that I am missing anything. That isn't a criticism of anyone who does participate in that way, just my way of believing that my faith is between me and the Lord, and no one else.

My belief now in God simply through faith is similar to a famous line from C.S. Lewis, the great writer from Northern Ireland. Lewis was a committed atheist as a young man, but ended up as one of the most important religious thinkers and writers of the twentieth century. These words are carved into his stone on the floor of the Poets' Corner in Westminster Abbey, London: "I believe in Christianity as I believe that the Sun has risen; not only because I see it, but because by it I see everything else."

EPILOGUE

All too often, the world seems to have gone mad these days. Perhaps it has always appeared that way, down through the ages, but the current environment has many believing the worst. I rely on faith now to sustain me through any madness.

Writing this memoir conjured up many memories for me, and some of those were very painful to relive. As a child and young man, I never really displayed much emotion. I rarely cried. Lying alone and awake in the dark of a polio ward, night after night as a four-year old will build that kind of stoicism. I find myself far more emotional today, reflecting not just on my life, but on events around me. Hearing stories of goodness, of acts of decency, or, most of all, of children struggling through physical problems can easily bring me to tears.

Red Smith, the famous sports writer, long ago commented, "Writing is easy. You simply sit down at the typewriter, open a vein, and bleed." I've certainly done my share of bleeding on my laptop writing this. It has not been easy revisiting some of the memories and moments, but in many ways, wonderfully cathartic.

As I write this and remember all that I've been through, I may not be done with physical challenges. Over 20 years ago, the medical world filled with stories about something called post-polio syndrome. A very real problem, which was then just widely surfacing. Survivors of polio who had overcome so much to live a normal life were finding themselves 30 or 40 years later suffering from muscle collapse and weakness, as if the original disease had returned. Some press accounts at the time estimated that a large percentage of those who originally had the disease, possibly up to 40 percent, would experience post-polio syndrome.

Naturally alarmed, I began researching whatever I could find. I read everything, attended a seminar put on by a local hospital chain, and finally talked to my doctor. He referred me to another doctor in their system, their expert on the subject. She and I were both polio survivors, so we had a very frank conversation.

She confirmed for me that although there were several theories as to the cause of post-polio, the most likely reason was a gradual failure of the muscle fibers and nerve cells that survived the original onslaught of the virus. The ones that survived either compensated, or overcompensated, for the dead muscles and nerves, and eventually wore out. There is no clear test for post-polio, and no treatment. She advised me to immediately stop actively participating in sports, and limit exercise to avoid over-stressing what I had left.

I ignored that advice and actually increased my active participation in everything. I told Kaye that if I was going out, I would go out on my terms, not those of some disease. She understood. I continued to do adventure travel, scuba diving all over the Caribbean and fishing the Florida Keys. I took my kayak to fish in the Sierra and southern Cascade mountains in California. I continued riding my bike everywhere. I traveled to new places in Mexico, Cuba twice, and back to Europe and Asia several times.

Things were fine physically until just a few years ago. It began with severe hip pain in my weaker leg. Then the pain spread sporadically down the leg to the thigh, knee, and ankle, matched by lower back pain and weakness. Some mornings, I was so weak and pain-wracked that I could hardly stand up. Had the wolf of polio truly come back again to stalk me?

I consulted with an orthopedic surgeon, a neurologist, a neurosurgeon, and a pain management doctor. Multiple X-rays and MRIs. An epidural shot in the back, steroidal injections in the hip, but nothing really helped much. The good news turned out to be that in their best judgment, I didn't have post-polio, which turned out to be rarer than originally thought. What I do have is a nasty combination of bursitis and osteoarthritis in my hip, coupled with stenosis and bulging discs in my lower back. Nerves are pinched off that lead down to my bad leg. Some of that is undoubtedly related to the fact that polio left my spine curved, due to one leg being much shorter than the other.

Although I am a candidate for serious back surgery, if things don't worsen, I can manage the pain and discomfort. Well, sort of. I gave away my kayak

and my ski gear, and the golf clubs might be next. At least I can still ride my bike. I am blessed.

Many times in life though, I have felt like Sisyphus. In *The Myth of Sisyphus,* Camus wrote of Sisyphus mastering his cruel fate: "There is no sun without shadow, and it is essential to know the night ... One always finds one's burden again ... The struggle itself toward the heights is enough to fill a man's heart. One must imagine Sisyphus happy." One must imagine me happy, too, except unlike Sisyphus, I never pushed my rock alone. After the journey of a lifetime, a journey of physical and emotional adventure, I know that now.

Ever since I was a little boy, I endured the same awkward question as soon as someone saw me walk. "What did you do to your leg?" When I was young, it was too painful to talk about polio, so I would mutter some answer like, "an accident as a child." More comfortable with the dreaded word in later years, I would simply say, "childhood polio." Invariably, the questioner would have a look of horror on their face, and usually try to apologize for asking. Now, I answer with, "I didn't do anything. God did."

Polio shaped my entire life, just as it misshaped my leg. It showed me the best in people, and at times, the worst. It made me feel empathy, compassion, and humility in ways I surely wouldn't have known without it. It led me to adventures and challenges that others would never have even attempted. Most importantly, it led me back to my faith. It took a lifetime for me to say this, but, thank God I got polio.

POSTSCRIPT—A SHORT STORY

The following short story by me was first published in <u>The Guilded Pen</u>, the annual anthology of the San Diego Writers and Editors Guild, in 2019, and since revised. It provides some context for the memoir.

Some Good People in the World

Flat, all right. He could stare at it all he wanted and the tire was just as flat. He had no other choice, so he left the Little League field on foot, pushing the Huffy bike. The flat tire flapped rhythmically in time with his steps.

Bobby thought it had enough air when he left home. It looked bad, but he was so anxious to watch his school buddies play a game that day that he risked it anyway.

"Darn it," he said aloud, "why didn't I fix this yesterday when it was already low?" He knew the answer, of course. He didn't know how to fix a flat tire. Dad fixed them for him many times, but Dad wasn't there. He was gone again, "on business," he was told.

Pushing the bike meant he'd have a very long and slow walk home. Up the big hill he didn't like riding and hated walking. Starting out, his leg flapped a little like the flat tire. By the time he reached home, he would be dragging the leg behind him.

The disease left that leg shrunken and weak. Surgeries and therapy made walking possible, but not done well. It was the bike that freed him from the stares of strangers, the occasional taunts, and the shame of inadequacy. On the bike, he moved like any other kid, with freedom. He was normal. And on the bike, he could escape them.

The apartment buildings across the street from the field were the first problem. Mean, hard people lived there. Whenever he passed by, it seemed

139

like someone was yelling. Bobby wanted to be on the other side of the street, except there was no sidewalk.

He moved past without incident, and continued up always busy Lemon Avenue. That wasn't a good place for him, either. Too many cars whenever he had to walk it. Sometimes older boys in a car would slow down just to yell insults when they saw his awkward gait. Bobby always wondered why. He didn't even know them, yet they felt the need to scream an insult while driving by.

That day was a good day. There were no passing cars. He made it to the quieter cross street, which wasn't pleasant even without traffic. Too many dogs barking and charging him, and he didn't know anyone on those blocks. At the end of the street, though, the reward of the junior high school, with its empty ballfields and frontage road usually blocked from traffic. There, he could continue the long march home alone. Unless they saw him. They might be there, waiting.

When he made it to the end of the block, Bobby scanned the vacant fields anxiously. He felt his usual dread while trying to walk quickly. Quickly really wasn't an option, but he scuttled along as fast as possible. No sign of them yet. Maybe he could hustle just a little more and escape notice this time.

He approached the outdoor equipment area with growing optimism. This was going to work; another glance at the fields revealed nothing. Two more blocks and he would be safely back in his own neighborhood.

Suddenly, there they were, emerging between two buildings. A pack of boys, maybe five or six. They headed to the pull-up bars, yelling and joking. As each one took to the bars, taunts from the others rang out over who could do the most.

Bobby froze with fear, hoping they wouldn't notice him. Where was his big brother? Big brother could take on all of them, Bobby just knew it. But he was alone, and running was out of the question. Head down, he started to move, very slowly.

"Hey, is that the cripple? That Bobby kid?"

"Yeah, I think it is. Let's mess him up more than he already is."

Bobby was quickly surrounded by the pack. One grabbed at his Huffy, then thrust it back, disgusted. "It's got a flat tire, just like him." The others roared with laughter.

The biggest boy moved in and gave Bobby a shove. "Whatcha doing here, anyway?"

"I'm, I'm t-trying just to, just to go home," was all he could choke out.

"So, what if we stop ya from going home? Whatcha gonna do about it?" he said, shoving Bobby again.

Another boy reached in and knocked Bobby's ball cap from his head just as the first rock crashed down on the leg of the boy in the rear. That boy screamed in pain, clutched his leg, and fell to the ground. The group spun around in panic as another rock thudded at their feet. One more granitic missile slammed into the biggest boy's thigh, who crumpled to the ground, crying.

Bobby looked up at the thrower, and right away recognized Corker. The bad older boy with the fabulous arm who had been kicked out of Little League a few years before.

"Leave him alone," Corker bellowed. They looked bewildered, some still whimpering. "Leave him alone," he yelled again, launching more rocks. When they hit at their feet, all of the boys turned and ran down the frontage road. One last missile skittered on the pavement between their legs.

Bobby wanted to yell his thanks, but he couldn't breathe. He tried again to shout, "thank you," and no words came out, so he just waved and waved. Corker made a casual half-wave back, and disappeared behind a building.

His limp didn't slow him as he almost skipped up the hill. He had a purpose; there was something to share. When he arrived home, his mother was working in the front yard.

"Hi, Bobby, how was the game? Bobby, are you OK? Your face looks flushed."

"I'm good, Mom. I'm really good."

"Well, you're excited. So, it was a good game, huh? Bobby, your tire's flat. How long has it been flat?"

"Since the ballpark."

"You walked all that way home? That must have been a tough walk."

"No, no, it was pretty easy. I didn't have any big problems. But, Mom?"

She turned away to keep him from seeing the tears welling in her eyes. She knew. There had been another incident. Why won't they leave him alone? What did he ever do to them?

"Bobby?"

"Mom, you know, there are some, uh, some good people in the world, right?"

"Yes. Yes, Bobby, there are. And, we'll get that tire fixed so you don't have to walk so much, OK?

POST-POSTSCRIPT—A NEWSPAPER ARTICLE

The following newspaper article about me was published in the San Diego Union-Tribune newspaper on June 17, 2011, and provides a little more context for the memoir.

This Papa Fishes From a Kayak

By Ed Zieralski, San Diego Union-Tribune

Ernest Hemingway would have liked Wayne Raffesberger, whose life was broadened and transformed a few years ago when he took up kayak fishing.

Raffesberger's return to fishing and his love of fishing alone in a Hobie kayak is the foundation for his plan to compete next month in a very special contest.

On July 21-23 Raffesberger will take his new fishing attitude and image and compete in the "Papa" Hemingway Look-Alike Contest at the famous Sloppy Joe's bar on Duval Street in Key West. Raffesberger will be judged by previous winners, champion look-alike Papas who will be looking for one guy who looks just like them. This year marks the 50th anniversary of Hemingway's suicide on July 2, 1961.

"I've never been a Hemingway freak," Raffesberger said. "But all of a sudden, a bunch of stuff came together, and I said, 'Hey this is fun. What the hell.'"

One of the things that sealed it for him was when his wife, Kaye, rescued a six-toed cat from an animal shelter. When he visited the Hemingway compound in Key West a few years ago, he saw descendants of the six-toed cat, polydactyls, that inhabited Hemingway's compound.

"We named the cat, a female, Ernie," Raffesberger said. "Kaye (his wife of 26 years) picked her out. The more I thought about it, the more I found myself driven to enter the contest."

He'd been a fisherman before, but had moved on to other diversions that tested his adventurous spirit. And what a spirit it is. It helped him overcome polio after it struck him when he was 4 years old. He underwent painful orthopedic surgeries that allowed him to live a life Hemingway would have admired.

"I really like being six inches from the water surface and just feeling a little bit more natural," said Raffesberger, whose 60th birthday is a few days after the "Papa" look-alike contest. "I don't have a big diesel motor chugging behind me or have to get into a line and then pick up a trailer afterward. I just put it on top of my SUV myself and go where I want to go, local lakes, the bay, the ocean, even the Sierra."

Win or lose, Raffesberger will dedicate his appearance in the contest to the late David Nuffer, a legendary public relations executive and civic leader in San Diego. Nuffer was a Hemingway expert who wrote a book, "The Best Friend I Ever Had," "Revelations about Ernest Hemingway from those who knew him."

Raffesberger will carry Nuffer's book to the audition and show the judging Papas what Hemingway looked like in a 1952 LIFE Magazine that ran Hemingway's entire "The Old Man and the Sea" inside. Kaye found the magazine among her mother's treasures.

"I don't have the white hair and white beard, but Hemingway didn't look like that when he was younger," Raffesberger said.

To play Hemingway, a look-alike has to have some of Papa's qualities, and Raffesberger does. His thirst for adventure led him to take a backpacking tour of the world after Stanford and USD law school.

He later took up long-distance bicycle racing, tennis, golf, scuba diving, snow skiing, parachuting and white water rafting. He caught piranha with a hand line in the Amazon, skied 22 miles down the Tasman Glacier in New Zealand, trekked in the Annapurna Range in Nepal, went diving in the Blue Hole in Belize and once dropped through an underwater cave to a depth of 150 feet beneath circling bull sharks.

He climbed Mount Kilimanjaro, Mount Whitney, Mount Rainier, Mount Shasta, and the Matterhorn. All this by a man who was stricken by polio as a 4-year-old, just months before Dr. Jonas Salk's polio vaccine was widely distributed. He was one of the first patients at Children's Hospital in San Diego. Doctors told he'd never walk again and would need the aid of braces and crutches. He proved them all wrong and dedicated his climb of Kilimanjaro to Children's Hospital and often has participated in fund-raising ventures for the hospital.

In addition to his many adventures, Raffesberger is a writer who has written articles and countless commentaries and editorials. He has been involved in the city's political scene since the late 1980s when he worked as a policy advisor for Ron Roberts when Roberts, now a County Supervisor, was a San Diego City Councilman. He also was chief of staff for San Diego City Councilman Tom Behr and lost his own bid for a council seat in 2002. He also was a volunteer director of Centre City Development Corp., and helped pave the way for the new location for the Monarch School.

These days when he's not fishing he's helping his father, Ray, and brother, Glenn, with the family's alternative energy business.

Before he competes in the Papa contest, Raffesberger will go diving at the Cayman Islands. He'll walk into Sloppy Joe's extra salty and looking and feeling like the most interesting man in the world, a lot like Papa.

(Reprinted with the permission of *The San Diego Union-Tribune*.)

ACKNOWLEDGMENTS

I have many to thank for helping me bring this book to life. First, my publisher, Waterside Productions, especially Josh Freel, Senior Publishing Associate. Ken Fraser of Impact Book Designs for the beautiful cover design. My editor, the brilliant Larry Edwards. Bill Corkery of Bill Corkery Productions for his always outstanding studio work on the audio version of the book. And finally, the many friends and family members who graciously participated in a manuscript beta group, and who offered their encouragement and constructive criticism. Their support and positive feedback through the long process truly kept me going.

ABOUT THE AUTHOR

Wayne Raffesberger is a freelance writer, voiceover talent, and all-around
raconteur. He has authored dozens of commentaries and opinion pieces that
have appeared in newspapers and magazines around the country. His short
stories have been published in local anthologies in San Diego, California,
and recognized in the international Lorian Hemingway Short Story Writing
Contest in Key West, Florida.

His work experience includes small business and land use attorney, political aide, executive director of business non-profits, business consultant, and
small businessman.

His hobbies include traveling, photography, fishing, biking, and an occasional game of golf. For the last decade, he has been a contestant in the annual
Ernest Hemingway Look-Alike Contest in Key West, Florida. He lives in San
Diego, California, with his wife, Kaye, and his six-toed cat, Ernie. As a poly-
dactyl, she is named after Ernest Hemingway, who had his own six-toed cats
while living in Key West.

Made in the USA
Columbia, SC
30 November 2021

50104532R00098